THE FINE ART OF FASHION ILLUSTRATION

THE FINE ART OF FASHION ILLUSTRATION

JULIAN ROBINSON
WITH GRACIE CALVEY

FASHION ILLUSTRATIONS FROM THE
JULIAN ROBINSON ARCHIVE

F

FRANCES LINCOLN LIMITED

CONTENTS

LEFT José Zinoview, *La Guirlande: Album d'Art et de Littérature*, hand-coloured pochoir, 1920

PREFACE AND DEDICATION

began collecting fashion images as a young, East London art student. What began as an antidote to the grim realities of the post-war years helped me to develop as a designer, an art school teacher and university lecturer, and later as a dealer, traveller and writer. It broadened my horizons in ways I never would have believed possible as a working class boy, born into the Depression of the 1930s. Over the sixty years or so of my professional life, I have had so many beautiful images, glimpses of a forgotten world, pass through my hands while searching and buying for myself, for other collectors, museums or art galleries and yet, such is their magic, that I feel I still know each one intimately.

No book can ever completely demystify the enchanting spell that many of these images project, just as no scientist, philosopher or artist will ever find an exact formula for the perfect female face or the ideal male body. Beauty is as elusive as it is multi-formed. Its infinite variety defies any generalization, but that has never stopped me trying to share the excitement I felt, and still feel, in the discovery and exploration of the wonderful world of fashion illustration and image-making.

Starting out as a juvenile film actor, I became an articled apprenticed craftsman, then a student at the Cordwainers and art school. After winning a Royal Scholarship at the Royal College of Art, I became a successful fashion designer, design consultant, collector and dealer. Later, I was Head of Design at several well-known art colleges and universities. Eventually, I got to weave these different career strands into my writing, producing books like *The Golden Age of Style, The Brilliance of Art Deco, The Fine Art of Fashion, The Quest for Human Beauty, Body Packaging – A Guide to Human Sexual Display* and many others. Most of my books have looked at aspects of our human fascination with body art and self-adornment.

RIGHT Carlos Bady, *La Journée de Mado*, hand-coloured pochoir, 1934

LEFT Pierre Louchel, *La Femme Chic*, photogravure, 1944

It was during the early years of the Second World War, at the height of the Blitz, that I first became interested in fashion and fashion illustration. I had been ill with rheumatic fever and found it impossible to run and play and take part in outdoor sports with my brothers. I had to spend most of my time indoors, watching my mother sew. To keep me amused she gave me scraps of fabric, beads and sequins and cut out fashion illustrations from her old scrapbooks. She started to teach me some hand-stitching, showing me more and more as I proved to have the nimble fingers for it. She thought perhaps I'd inherited the aptitude from herself and her grandfather, who had been a respected gentlemen's tailor before the First World War.

By comparison to this world of fashion drawings and soft fabrics, school was a nightmare. In 1930s Britain, particularly in 1930s working class Britain and more especially in the East End of London, school was a machine for churning out manual workers, who on the whole knew just enough to work and know their place in a somewhat rigid society. I was painfully shy. I also couldn't see the board and, when I could, nothing made sense. I later discovered I was dyslexic, but at the time I was just considered to be a dunce. I couldn't spell, couldn't read and, although I was good with numbers, couldn't follow the normal methods used for arriving at the correct answer, which led to my being accused of cheating and given the obligatory punishment. The one upside to being considered 'dull' was that when a film company came looking for extras and child actors, the teachers were quite happy to allow me to go whenever required on the set. When not involved in a film, I began to play truant, spending whole days exploring. I took the canings and punishments, but I continued to escape, more often than not, until I was finally forced to leave school, rather ignominiously. I was caned in front of the whole school, again for truancy and with an extra 'six of the best' for crying. My parents were summoned by the headmaster, who informed them that I was being expelled, that I was unteachable, would never read or write to 'any reasonable extent' and that he saw very little hope for me in the future, except as a 'farmhand or manual labourer'. It was one of the happiest days of my life. I learned very early that what others may consider a handicap or a burden – being a sick child, being dyslexic, being caned and expelled – can actually work in quite another way. Looking back, I think I can trace some of my love of illustration to my being dyslexic. An image can speak volumes, to the heart and mind, without the need for a single word. It is somewhat ironic that in trying to promote fashion, human adornment and the art of their depiction, I became a writer.

Being an accidental academic, I had a need to collect the earliest examples I could find, to understand and make understandable to students the development of fashion, fashion Illustration and the publications that dealt with the subject. In so doing I was lucky to come across a copy of the 1590s Venetian bestseller, *Habiti Antichi*, and a number of other early woodcuts and rare fashion publications, adding examples from every period over the years to demonstrate how fashion and fashion media evolved.

Since closing my fashion business and resigning from the university, I have travelled widely and lived in some of the most remote areas of the world, continuing my collecting, broadening its scope – researching tribal adornments and all forms of body modification. Everywhere I have been, I have found clear evidence that we all share the same aesthetic need to play with our appearance, to make ourselves beautiful or interesting – be that among the Wodaabe, the Maasai, the Akha, the peoples of the Highlands of Papua New Guinea or the tribes of Bobos, Preppies, Punks, Skinheads, Goths or Hipsters to be found closer to home. We do it now and we have always done so. All over the world, I have found what are basically fashion images – painted on rock faces in the Australian tropics, in Egyptian tombs, on Grecian pottery, Minoan and Roman walls, carved in Assyrian or Aztec stone – finds that indicate a very deeply embedded desire, maybe even an evolutionary need, in all of us for an aesthetic expression, both general and personal, of our creative differences.

Fashion illustrations wordlessly carry within them so much information, both historical and cultural. For far too long, they have been overlooked by art and history academics, but even a cursory inspection of a fashion print can bring to life a particular period in ways no amount of text can manage – a fashion drawing can give a glimpse of manners and customs at play and it can show us which aesthetic ideals were aspired to and by whom. They often give clues to the wider events of the day and the consequent feelings of the people involved. The study of fashion illustration through the ages now has a place as an important source, these days called material culture, for historians, ethnographers and scientists, as it always has for fashion designers, costume designers, filmmakers, artists, connoisseurs and collectors.

All of this having been said, I must add that this book would not have been possible without the help and support of my partner and co-author, Gracie Calvey, who has patiently worked her way through our archives (learning and researching and adding to it as she went), painstakingly deciphering my reams of dyslexic text and joining her words to mine in a way that has made the often difficult task of writing as a team thoroughly enjoyable. She has, together with help from our editor, Nicki Davis, turned my life of collecting into a treasure trove of images and information that hopefully does some justice to this fascinating world of fashion illustration. And, while I am delighted that the subject, which has engaged me for so many years, is now being taken seriously, our book has a less weighty, but no less worthy, intention. It is a book about pleasure – dreams of the past as revealed in fashion illustrations, designed, in their day, to please the eyes and stimulate the imaginations of all who saw them . . . and you, dear Reader, are the latest in a very long line of appreciative eyes to see the images that follow. We therefore dedicate this book to your enjoyment. We wish you pleasant reading but, more importantly, pleasurable looking and inspired seeing.

Julian Robinson.

RIGHT *La Femme Chic*, pochoir and lithograph, 1912

La Femme "Chic"

Supplément

N.º 12   Pl. 120

J.Bas,Imp.Paris

Toilette d'après-midi

Création Martial & Armand

INTRODUCTION

This book is a visual celebration of more than four hundred years of the fine art of fashion illustration, as seen through the work of many skilled and talented artists and craftsmen. The images you see here have been selected from those created for books, folders and magazines, printed and published across the centuries – from the Renaissance to the years immediately following the Second World War. Most are the result of the coming together of two talents – those of the creative artist and the interpretative craft of a great engraver or woodcutter. They represent some of the most poignant, memorable and aesthetically pleasing fashion illustrations ever published. Our hope is that by bringing them together in a single volume they will be appreciated as individual pieces of art, as windows into their time and as a testament to our species' endless fascination with difference and personal style.

Fashion illustration is an ancient art, perhaps the oldest of all art forms, with its origins only now being hinted at by recent discoveries. Of particular importance in this regard are the painted prehistoric figures currently being researched in north-west Australia, which are thought to have been made by an unknown, possibly transient, people during the last Ice Age. These beautiful rock paintings, known as the Bradshaws after the British explorer who discovered them in the nineteenth century, clearly depict a people for whom a fashion for elaborate hairstyles and tasselled garments was important and worthy of record. These may well be the oldest existing fashion images ever found and together with others, sculpted or painted by artists and craftsmen of practically every people of the ancient world – the Sumerians, the Assyrians, Incas, Minoans, Egyptians, Greeks, Celts and Romans – they show that the shape and surface detailing we call fashion is a very ancient, very human preoccupation. It appears to run

LEFT René Hermann-Paul, *Le Calvaire*, pochoir and woodcut, 1928

deeper than the usual historical and aesthetic analysis allows. From tentative prehistoric beginnings, our fascination with clothing and self-decoration seems to have developed as an integral part of who we are, evolving along natural pathways of change and difference, little by little, influencing our cultures and possibly our physical bodies as well.

Fashion itself is a powerful language that allows one to broadcast one's affiliations and aspirations, to marry the spiritual, inner self to the outside world. Clothes of one sort of cut or colour can make one a knight or a knave, while other choices of fabrics or trimmings can paint one a saint or a sinner. In short, clothes and fashion have the power to transform; they allow us to express who we truly are or to become something totally 'other'. If fashion is a coded message that spells out something about the wearer, then fashion illustration might be akin to a poem written in that language. Like poetry, fashion and fashion illustration have a special attraction for us and while neither poetry nor adornment appears to be absolutely essential for everyday living, we cherish them for the spark of creativity and magic they bring to our lives.

The human race – at least that part lucky enough to live in relative comfort and security – is concerned not just with survival, but with

TOP Ancient Grecian frieze, marble haut-relief, from the Parthenon, 400 BCE ABOVE LEFT Assyrian archer, stone bas-relief, 700–600 BCE ABOVE RIGHT Lady of Elche, Iberian limestone carving, fifth century BCE

passion and desire and no art form comes closer to those concerns than fashion. It touches us, literally, more closely than anything else – after all, we wear it on our skin. Sciences, law, medicine are all noble and invaluable pursuits which help keep us alive, but fashion and fashion images, in all their various forms, provide us with an irresistible cocktail of beauty, sensuality, allure, romance and personal power, and these are things we stay alive for. This book is about such allure and beauty, as captured by artists, well known and nameless, who, working alone or hand in hand with talented printmakers, created a genre of art and information sharing that grew via black and white printed penny sheets and journals into glorious full-colour fashion magazines, eventually becoming today's digital and paper publications. Many of the featured illustrations, surprisingly, have not been republished since their first appearance. Our aim is to bring some of them back into the light of public attention, and so this book is designed as a visual celebration of a much neglected art – an art form that, during its four hundred years of pre-eminence, inspired many talented artists. These beautiful images were created in response to a growing public demand for illustrative and creative design material that began during the latter years of the Renaissance and the beginning of the Age of Discovery. This was the era that finally put an end to serfdom throughout most of Western Europe and to the centuries of cultural stagnation, brutality and ignorance that had been punctuated only by wars and crusades since the decline of the Roman Empire.

ABOVE Drawing from Egyptian tomb painting, line block, nineteenth century
RIGHT Egyptian tomb painting, *c*.1300 BCE

LEFT Henry Moses, Greek lady, engraved for Thomas Hope's *Costumes of the Ancients*, 1809
RIGHT George Barbier, *Le Journal des Dames et des Modes*, hand-coloured pochoir, 1913

At the start of this period, few dared question the rightness of the rule of kings or the power of the medieval Church, with all of its inherent ignorance, roughness, violence and armoury of persuasive punishments. Few dared doubt that the Earth lay motionless at the centre of the universe, which itself was said to be controlled by a single, and resolutely Christian, god. During the fifteenth century, this belief began to change and with this change came new ideas about personal freedom, lifestyle and how individuals could, and should, dress and present themselves to the world. This was a golden period, a time when modern ideas about everything from freedom – generally and particularly – to art and science, class and money were born. Out of that search for freedom came a burning interest in fashionable dress and ornamentation as an indicator of all of the above and, consequently, a new and abiding interest in fashion illustration.

Few eras in our history and in the development of western art and our cultural and aesthetic sensibilities had gotten off to such a dramatic and fortuitous start as that of the Renaissance. This was a time of unparalleled creative energy, enthusiasm, collaborative enterprise and intellectual excitement, when aesthetic experimentation, bravura risk-taking and information technology combined to spread word of voyages and discoveries far and wide, setting the western world on its ear and fueling the imagination of artists and creatives for generations.

LEFT George Barbier, *Falbalas et Fanfreluches*, hand-coloured pochoir, 1921

It also signaled the beginning of the end of the medieval power of the Church and hereditary autocrats and their world view, replacing it with an essentially modern outlook.

Today, the Renaissance brings to mind a litany of illustrious names – artists like Giotto and Dürer, Botticelli, Raphael, Titian and da Vinci, whose painted images blossom before our eyes – images so ingrained in our culture that marketers still deploy them to sell everything from a tube of toothpaste to a printed T-shirt. The word means 'rebirth', coined to signify a period in our cultural history when there was a notable change in the social order, the individual's sense of their place in the world and a revived interest in the arts and letters of ancient Greece and Rome. This would launch the beginnings of a humanist movement in the seventeenth century, reflecting a new conviction in the natural dignity of man and a blossoming of aesthetic values, including those related to forms of human adornment, that helped create the society that was, eventually, to find its counterpart in modern Europe.

This new social order had its roots in independent cities and city states like Venice, Milan, Genoa and Florence, which in the mid-to-late fifteenth century, after the fall of Constantinople and the Byzantine Empire to the Ottomans, were strategically placed along the trade routes to the East, with well-established access to the rest of Europe. These cities had grown rich on this trade, developing flourishing rural and urban lifestyles that had little in common with the feudal societies of the Middle Ages. In addition to trading in silks, spices, ivory, gold and a wide and varied assortment of eastern luxury goods, these newly emerging, wealthy middle class citizens became involved in banking, politics and all manner of financial and commercial undertakings, including investment in new and costly overseas exploration. Their acceptance of commercial risks, their changing political views, their scheming and adventures, their power and riches, plus their growing refinement of taste and culture – together constitute a break from the constricting and dehumanizing net that had formed and contained most European medieval societies for close on a thousand years.

During this period, contact with visiting traders from the Ottoman Empire and the great trading cities of Damascus, Cairo, Baghdad and the Far East began to influence the dress styles of European merchants and travellers. As individual wealth grew, merchants, along with their wives and families, began to refine their taste, using their wealth to better their appearance, improving sales of silks, patterned damasks or jewellery by dressing their wives and daughters in fashionable, enviable clothes designed to show off the merchandise. Consequently, as the wealth of these communities increased, so the number of artists and artisans exploded to cater for the growing demand for portraits, accessories and furnishings capable of showcasing their clients' position, wares and belongings.

To boost their chances of employment or to gain a commission, these artists and craftsmen had to be inventive and pay close attention to important and telling details. Most of them were trained from an early age as an apprentice, often working years without remuneration, until they were accomplished enough to start their own studio or win a place in a noted or reputable atelier. For a child born into a craft-oriented family or one involved in the visual arts, that meant starting to work as soon as they were able to understand simple tasks. Such a child was expected to hone their skills to become successful in 'doing', not 'knowing'. The knowing would come later, after they had perfected the art of seeing and doing and could contribute a profit to the atelier and the work of their master, becoming craftsmen or artisans in their own right.

The history of the visual arts – which includes fashion illustration, as well as the arts of printmaking, engraving and painting – is made up of skilled craftsmen who learned this art of seeing and doing, not discussing or theorizing, but seeing clearly and rendering what their eyes and mind's eye saw, fulfilling the demands of their patrons and clients. Today, we are generally taught from books or lectures. We are not taught to see, rarely to do, but rather to look and to think. Being able to see is very different. The contemporary artist David Hockney, in his landmark book and documentary *Secret Knowledge*, explained that 'learning how to draw and paint with any sort of skill and accuracy – learning how to coordinate what you see with what you are drawing, for me, it was four years of sitting and drawing. Only after sitting and drawing, day after day, was I able to see what I was really looking at.'

The art of seeing and being skilled enough to successfully translate that vision had particular value at the start of the Renaissance, when painters were simply artisans. With the changes that this new period would bring, some of these artisans would transform, becoming artists. Dürer is an excellent example. Born in 1471, in Nuremberg, to a family of skilled craftsmen, he was the son of a successful Hungarian goldsmith, with whom he began his aesthetic and technical training several years before officially becoming an apprentice. From about six years old, it was clear that Dürer had an exceptional, precocious talent for drawing.

Through his family's connections, the young Dürer was exposed to the cutting edge of thought, invention and technology sparked by the Renaissance and disseminated broadly, and faster than ever before, by the revolutionary leaps forward in printing. He was at the heart of one of the first information revolutions in human history, Nuremberg being one of the main centres for the radical changes in the print industry, as well as one of the great luxury goods markets of Europe. Importantly, it also had strong links to that other, perhaps greater, printing centre, Venice. For a young and obviously gifted mind, the effect must have been huge. In three years, the student, already skilled in the use of fine goldsmithing tools, would outstrip his apprenticeship master. With his mastery of the tools of two trades, his powerful talent and aesthetic sense, and being in the right places at the right time, Dürer was ideally placed to appreciate how best to profit from his gift and used his work to position and promote himself in fashionable society.

During this time, many of those in the growing middle class, the merchants and traders and the attendant skilled workers – from tailors, weavers, shoe-makers, perfumers, dress-makers and inventors through to soldiers for hire – began experimenting with the possibility of presenting themselves differently to the world. Like Dürer, many began to use a fashionable appearance to woo clients and upgrade their social position. They used the skills of their tailors, dress-makers, shoe-makers, furriers, their barbers and hairdressers to project a suitable image of themselves and their families and then employed portrait artists to capture and embellish their appearance in paint, for all to see. They were now all part of the growing world of fashion and image-making – tools once only available to the upper echelons were now available to those with new money rather than blue blood. Artists were employed as craftsmen in the service of those richer than themselves, their products being comparatively inexpensive compared to those of the tailors, dress-makers and the exotic fabric merchants. This meant they could be commissioned to use their highly trained imaginations, painting details that didn't exist to confer status and style, attributes previously determined by the accidental gift of an aristocratic birth, but which could now be bought by anyone with enough money to spend. Artists thus became part of the growing world of consumerism and were essential to the new and lucrative need for 'image enhancement' and self-presentation. This use of clothes and art as tools to define themselves in new ways aided in the development of individuality. It offered a way out of the conformity of the past – a powerful freedom.

In 1530, the first book of 50 woodcut images of the German Landsknecht and the Swiss mercenary soldiers involved in the Italian wars and the Turkish seige of Vienna was published in Nuremberg by Nicolaus Meldemann and Hans Guldenmundt. The illustrations started with a woodcut of the Emperor Maximillian I, dated 1508, and

LEFT George Vertue, *Elizabeth I*, engraving, 1700s

continued with 49 single-page woodcut depictions of widely differing and formalized slashed uniforms. The second and third volumes of this remarkable collection were published in 1540 and 1550, featuring between them 150 images showing dress styles that were adopted by wealthy merchants and entrepreneurs, adding to the erosion of the previously rigid sumptuary laws. The series was so popular that all three volumes were eventually combined in 1560 as *Kreigsbuch des Grafen Reinhart zu Solms*.

In 1543, Pope Paul II created the Index of Prohibited Books, curtailing the range of book production. In searching for new markets and new areas of interest that could avoid running foul of the papal rules, publishers quickly spotted a niche in the public's hunger for books on differing dress forms and fashions from all over known and New World. In 1568, Jost Amman published his well-illustrated *Book of Trades* and followed it in 1574 with his *Costumes of the Nations of the World*, again with many fine woodcut illustrations. But it was in 1587 that he created his most celebrated book, *Gynaeceum; or The Theatre of Women*, which contained many woodcuts illustrating 'the female costumes of all the principal nations, tribes and peoples of Europe' – a book that many regard as a key publication in the history of fashion illustration. In 1577, one of the first books to detail differing European clothing styles appeared – the *Trachtenbuch*. It was illustrated by the German woodcut artist Hans Weigel and published by Sigmund Feyerabend, the leading entrepreneurial publisher of the day, with 219 single-page woodcuts in full quarto format with captions in German and Latin. Though popular, this book, like several others of the period, lacked the necessary artistic magic to inspire the public's desire for new fashions. That was left to to the Venetian painter Cesare Vecellio and his book *De gli Habiti Antichi et Moderni di Diverse Parti del Mondo*, published in 1590s Venice. *Habiti Antichi* was a revelation to those concerned with the growing interest in changeable dress styles, both men and women of the new wealthy merchant class. Such preoccupations were comparatively new in 1590 and were widely criticized by an array of clerics, both Catholic and Protestant, despite the fact that members of the Church hierarchy were not averse to ostentatious display themselves.

This was a time of change throughout Europe. In England, it was the beginning of the Golden Age of Elizabeth I. The threat of the Spanish Armada had dissipated and both Christopher Marlowe and William Shakespeare were busy at work. New discoveries were being made in Africa, the Americas and around the world and new maps were being published, showing that the Earth was truly round and that the peoples who lived in these newly discovered regions had different cultures and ideas about morality and modes of dress. But this was also a time when different ideas could be dangerous. The Pope's edict on book burning was still in force, and in Rome Giordano Bruno was burnt at the stake for attempting to publish a book on the infinite cosmos he had observed through the newly invented telescope, while his friend Galileo was threatened by the Inquisition with both torture and death by burning if he dared publish his observations on the true structure of the universe.

The growing hunger for knowledge and books was provoking some strong reactions from those in charge. Vecellio's book, however, together with those of Jost Amman, Hans Weigel and that other remarkable traveller and recorder of difference, Nicolas de Nicolay, being all, seemingly, just books of pretty pictures of clothes, slipped through the Church's net to become publishing sensations. They were all destined, in their own way, to provoke deep changes in the social order and even to affect the stability of those twin bastions of control – Church and State. By the close of the sixteenth century, information spread far and wide, thanks to books and printed images. Nothing could stem the thirst for new ideas. The need for freedom of thought and expression, the desire to understand and question grew until neither censorship nor papal edicts, not even the Inquisition and pain of death, could fully stamp it out. The printed word allowed those

LEFT Mario Simon, *La Gazette du Bon Ton*, hand-coloured pochoir, 1920
RIGHT Eduardo García Benito, *La Gazette du Bon Ton*, hand-coloured pochoir, 1921

of like mind to communicate and organize sweeping changes until, by the end of the 1590s, the one religion that had defined European life since the fall of the Roman Empire had been challenged and, in some countries, even replaced altogether. Attitudes to religion having shifted so dramatically, a change in people's perception of, and deference to, that other untouchable, royalty, became noticeable. Eventually in England, these new concepts would lead a society to try a king, execute him for treason, and sew abroad the seeds for future revolutions far from their own shores.

Fashion is about such transformations – seemingly simple acts of embellishing appearances, and inspiring dreams of difference, are actually anything but. And to understand why this hitherto neglected art of change must now form an important part of the new cultural history of the western world, this book explores, through pictures, the ways in which men and women, across society and across time, gave

meaning to their world through personal visual statements, created in a myriad of ways – practices that changed or challenged conventions and laws. It opens in an era of dramatic social change, fueled by the growing efficiency of printing techniques, the rapid diffusion of knowledge, an increasing use of printed images and of vernacular language, a rising literacy rate in many urban centres – when a new and powerful interest in secular subjects began, despite angry Church opposition, to impact on the public's imagination and aspirations.

This book celebrates the presence of the future in these images and the inspiring effect they had on their original observers – promoting a way of dressing, a way of living, a way of seeing and being seen in the world. From its earliest beginnings, the fashion illustration encapsulated dreams and wishes in a way that, later, fashion photography never could. Photography reflects and records what already exists – illustration has no such restraint. Fashion illustrations can link distant cultures, bring together materials from opposite ends of the planet and inspire a vision of the future, or the past, all with an intuitive stroke of the pen or brush.

Today, we are used to seeing photographs of the 'latest fashion', but we rarely get a glimpse of what might have been. The magazine photo-spreads are of existing clothes already in the distribution pipeline, part of the great modern machine of mass production and the homogenized commercialism of the 'Now'. The photographers and magazine editors have become the real trendsetters. The driving force no longer flows from the creative talent of designers or illustrators nor from the aesthetic and self-expressive aspirations of customers. It is big business – a world of bottom-lines, cost-paring and outsourcing, homogenized designs suitable for the widest possible demographic and the largest, fastest turnover. Unfortunately, the real forces behind most of today's trends are the holders of the purse strings to the media advertising budgets.

Prior to 1950, creative forms and styles of fashion illustration were still widely used, part of the highly skilled aesthetic process that characterised fashion, from concept to finished product, up to that point. In the years following the end of the Second World War and the introduction of Christian Dior's 'New Look', a process of commercialization (described as democratization) began. Dior was the earliest couturier to go with the wave of change, selling his original designs directly to manufacturers around the world. At the same time, photographs, with the introduction of new high-speed cameras and new colour film, began to replace illustration with glamorized colour photographs. A new generation of university graduate fashion editors, trained in words, not images, demanded more control, opting for the safer, more predictable results afforded by photography in place of the idiosyncratic, sometimes esoteric, eye of an illustrator. Increasingly, the editor's role was to please the advertisers and sell their merchandise.

The Fine Art of Fashion Illustration is about ideas and ideals and the constant search for those pleasures of the eye that arouse our most intimate senses – the pleasure that comes from the slight differences and nuances between variations of silhouette and details of line and fit – the use of textured fabrics, lace and ribbons, the placing of buttons, or the wearing of rare and expensive feathers as coded signals. It's about hemlines, shoes, lingerie and the appeal of jewellery. This book is not about fashion imagery as a documentary tool for recording historical costume, but as aesthetic images in their own right, as visually appealing and challenging as they are socially significant. These are unique images that speak eloquently and powerfully for themselves and about the art of appearance and difference that was an important, even a driving force, in society's progress.

In the 21st century, those of us lucky enough to live in areas of the planet with ample resources and opportunity live the legacy of those days, surrounded by information, ideas and imagery available at the push of a button. Nothing else charts the journey from who we were to who we have become more clearly than the skilful work of the image-makers featured in the following pages, who, between the mid-sixteenth and mid-twentieth centuries, captured the hopes and dreams of their contemporaries and, from them, distilled the lingering essence of their respective eras.

This book is a unique treasure trove of the very best images from our extensive personal collection, some of which have remained in obscurity since their first printing. They have been reproduced here from those original publications and they recall all the changes, dreams and wishes of talented artists across those centuries, from Cesare Vecellio, Claude-Louis Desrais, François-Louis-Joseph Watteau, Nikolaus Wilhelm von Heideloff and Rudolph Ackermann to Charles Martin, George Barbier, Paul Iribe, Pierre Mourgue, Bernard Blossac, Etienne Drian, Armand Vallée, Eduardo García Benito, Umberto Brunelleschi and many, many others. These images reveal aspects of our past and the history of various societies and are now, rightly, considered to be an important historical source – a witness to the characteristics and mores of their particular epoch. This use of fashion and its imagery, as a way to retrospectively understand how people of previous ages saw, felt and presented themselves in the face of the events of their day, is fast becoming a fertile area for professional research, attracting curators, ethnographers, art critics

LEFT *Deutsche Moden-Zeitung*, offset lithograph, 1940

and historians of all sorts, as well as serving as a source of inspiration for filmmakers, costumiers and design professionals of all kinds. It is a resource that nourishes their imaginations and widens their field of creativity.

This, then, is not an art history or a social history or even a history of fashion, although a little background is enlightening. Nor is it a book about the commercialization of fashion or the rise of fashion photography. It is, quite simply, an invitation to look at the work of these talented artists not as commercial fashion images or historical costume records, but as images in their own right. It is a luxurious collection of original fashion images, by many famous artists and talented illustrators, published in quality magazines, journals, folders and books that tell stories of their time. Unique and idealized images of desire, they can be read as coded messages of change and freedom, as well as being viewed as simply beautiful.

As with all art forms, fashion illustration has had its creative periods and its lean times – times of triumph and opulence and times of paucity and patchy quality – and, as with other art forms, the best individual pieces can stand alone on their own merit. To this end, the illustrations in this book aren't organized in a strictly linear way, with various periods overlapping so that their distinctive aesthetic qualities become more evident. They are identified simply by the name of the artist, the publication and date (where known), leaving the illustration to be appreciated purely for itself, not for any intellectual associations.

This book is a celebration of our humanness and our inborn desire for change and difference of all kinds, not for any rational reason, but purely because they highlight what is at the core of all our aesthetic endeavours – a search for pleasures of the eye, free from all forms of intellectualism or educated understanding – simply, the pleasure achieved by looking and seeing.

The three hundred or so illustrations that appear were culled from our extensive archives of books, folders, journals and magazines. It was a difficult process – weighing the merits of one image against another. Which could possibly represent the best of each generation's style and spirit? We looked for images that had a particular, evocative visual magic. The library floor has been littered with pictures, all clamouring for attention, enough to fill a dozen books or more, but publishing and printing restrictions require hard choices to be made and, in the end, this is a personal selection which we hope will spark further interest in a fascinating subject and, above all, please and delight both the intellect and the eye.

CHAPTER ONE
THE RENAISSANCE

Our story of fashion illustration, the ultimate art of transformation, begins in a very different time and world to our own – one of exploration, expansion, experimentation, new discoveries, new wealth and innovative ideas.

Today, we associate the Renaissance period with a revival of classical influences in literature and the arts of painting, sculpture and architecture. It was also a time where, thanks to a burgeoning trade in silk and damask fabrics and novelties from the Ottoman Empire, the Far East and the New World, those with means and position could indulge in conspicuous spending, reinventing themselves, proving their worth and improving their position with the creation of intricately decorated 'show' homes filled with highly embellished personal items, commissioned portraits and paintings and in the wearing of enviably fashionable garments.

The early Renaissance saw the birth of mechanized printing, the introduction of reusable, moveable type and of multiple printing of engraved and woodcut images in books of all descriptions, including those on the wide variety of differing modes of dress and alternative ways of adorning the human body with ideas gleaned from newly discovered lands and cultures.

The development of the mechanical printing press and of printable paper enabled the artisan printer to combine text and images in the same printing plate, producing books on a scale unimaginable during the previous centuries. Even in the early 1400s, fashionable books of the time, such as the various editions of the Book of Hours, were entirely handmade by skilled craftsmen and artisans. Every page of

LEFT Jacques de Gheyn II, *Vanitas: Young Woman with a Mirror*, steel engraving, 1596 such a book was individually designed and painstakingly written and illustrated by a skilled specialist, with each page being cut from a sheet of natural vellum or parchment, tanned from the skins of sheep or calves – each skin yielding around eight small, double-sided pages. One such Book of Hours, *Les Très Riches Heures du Duc de Berry*, took years of painstaking work to be complete to the satisfaction of the purchaser and, like all such handmade and painted books, it was a special commission and was never repeated. This was true for many similar vellum books that were created in the hundred years from 1350.

By the mid-1450s, after many difficult years of experimentation, the era of the one-off book was coming to an end, to be replaced by mechanically printed books. Woodcut-block printing of images, with the accompanying text being carved, letter by letter, in reverse, onto a single block of cross-grain hardwood, page by page, had arrived in various European trading cities from China during the early fourteenth century. A new time-saving adaptation was developed by the German printer and publisher Johannes Gutenberg in Mainz. In 1455, using his invention of moveable, resettable metal type, he successfully fulfilled his first print order using the new handmade paper. His first orders came from the Vatican for a quantity of Indulgences, which were sold throughout Europe in exchange for the Pope's automatic 'Forgiveness of Sin' – a venture that netted a fortune.

For a while, Gutenberg and his partner Petrus Schoeffer had the field to themselves, no doubt because their workers were sworn to secrecy. Soon, however, the secret was out and presses, with new refinements like intaglio printing, were at work in cities like Nuremberg, Venice and Mainz. Forms of stenciling were also used in printing workshops for colouring areas of design – adapted from those used since the fourteenth century to make Tarot cards. Some used specially cut coarse-grained woodblocks with coloured inks for distinctive effects. Within twenty-five years of its introduction, the printing press had spawned a huge and growing industry. As demand for their products increased, skills learned in one printing method were mixed with others and new experimental techniques were continually being developed and adapted. Albrecht Dürer was an apprentice during this exciting period to one of the most renowned printers in Nuremberg, Michael Wolgemut, and had perfected all of the then known methods for use in his own work. He understood that, like all other artisans and craftsmen of that period, his worth depended on skill, and that all commissioned work had to be carried out to a standard and to a brief, acceptable to the client, before payment would be made. Our current idea that artists were free spirits who could indulge in

RIGHT Albrecht Dürer, *Noblewoman at Horse and Landsknecht*, woodcut, *c.*1490

LEFT Albrecht Dürer, *The Masquerade*
from *Freydal*, woodcut, *c*.1510

aesthetic masterpieces as they saw fit was not known by Dürer or any
other artisan, printer, engraver, illustrator or sculptor who worked
for their living during the Renaissance. Dürer, like many artisans
who followed him, had the intelligence, the experience and the all
important aesthetic skill to combine everything he was taught in his
work, giving his images that extra element of 'fashionability' still
present in his woodcuts and self-portraits some five hundred years
later.

Dürer's work was influenced by the latest in everything, from
ideas, books and technology to clothes, fabrics and luxury goods from
far flung places. His love of the new and the fashionable is especially
obvious in the self-portraits he painted at this time. In these portraits,
he used his seemingly casual but carefully put together look to impress
potential clients, even employing a specialist to regularly wave and
curl his hair. These paintings, of a young man fully aware of the power
of fashion and confident in his use of the arts of self-promotion and
self-expression through dress, show him as a consummate fashion
illustrator and arbiter of taste. He showcases the clothes and, through
the clothes, the mood and mind of the wearer and of the time. Because
of this, he is perhaps the first widely published fashion illustrator, the
creator of the genre.

Instinctively, Dürer identified the effect that changeable fashion
was going to have on the art and aesthetics of painting and the new

print media. He had seen how woodcut images had improved book production, contributing to the ever faster spread of new ideas and tastes. He had also witnessed the first real example of how print media could impact on fashion. It came at the end of the fifteenth century, with the publication of a number of printed woodcut images showing the fashion for slashing, as invented by German and Swiss mercenaries. Myth has it that this 'Landsknecht' style began when these soldiers captured a quantity of colourful silks and velvets. They were cut into strips and patches to repair and decorate their own tattered clothing, and they pulled the strips of bright fabric through various slashings and holes. It was a very novel style of dress, with the added spice of flouting the sumptuary laws that still existed, and it quickly spread to all strata of society despite commentators like Erasmus declaring that 'clothing that has been slashed apart suggests madness'. Regardless, rulers, such as Henry VIII and Henry, Duke of Saxony and his wife, were painted in such garments – formalized, by their tailors and dress-makers, into works of art, displaying several hundred neatly sewn slashes over coloured linings, setting a style to be followed by courtiers of the English, French, Spanish and other European courts. From tattered mercenaries to kings and courtiers ... quite possibly the first example of 'street fashion' filtering upwards.

By 1510, Dürer was working in the service of the Emperor Maximilian, for whom he designed and made many woodcut illustrations, including the epic *Freydal*, the history of his masquerades and tournaments. Unlike most other woodcut artisans of the period, Dürer achieved a remarkable freedom of line in his renderings that set him apart. His works were immediately popular and were reprinted in Venice, Basel, Mainz, Nuremberg, Cologne, Strasbourg as well as London, Paris, Utrecht, Antwerp and other European cities. He became one of the early stars of an information revolution and all over Europe young artists, seeing his work, strove to emulate him.

A book depicting the distinctive dress of the Landsknecht mercenary soldiers, each in variations of the flamboyantly slashed costumes for which they had become famous, was being prepared at the same time as *Freydal. Kriegsvolker im Zeitalter der Landsknechte*, published in 1530, contains 50 beautifully drawn original designs, printed from woodcuts made in the 1520s. It is a treasure trove of fashion ideas, involving slashes of the kind reinvented by the 1970s Punk styles. This, and the subsequent two volumes that followed – in all, 150 variations on a theme, a parade of interchangeable detail and ideas – are sometimes regarded as the first true fashion catalogue.

At the same time, several small books with fine woodcut illustrations by Jost Amman appeared. The most notable, entitled *Gynaeceum; or*

ABOVE LEFT & RIGHT Jörg Breu the Elder,

Kriegsvolker im Zeitalter der Landsknechte,

woodcut, 1520s

RIGHT Peter Flötner, *Kreigsbuch des Grafen Reinhart*

zu Solms, woodcut, 1535

LEFT Jost Amman, *Gynaeceum; or Theatre of Women*, hand-coloured woodcut, 1586

ABOVE LEFT TO RIGHT Jost Amman, *Das Standebuch*, woodcut, 1568

The Theatre of Women, which featured 'All the Female Costumes of all the Principal Nations, Tribes and Peoples of Europe', was published in Frankfurt and is regarded by many as the first popular book on fashion illustration. Born in Zurich in 1539, Amman came from a well educated family and was encouraged to travel widely in his late teens, before starting an apprenticeship in Nuremberg with Virgil, a disciple of Dürer. Most of his work was published by the entrepreneur Sigmund Feyerabend – the leading publisher of his day and one of the major figures in the establishment of the internationally known European book fair, still held every October in Frankfurt. Amman went on to produce several books of interest – *Das Standebuch* (Book of Trades), *Kunst und Lerbuchlein* (a collection of prints for the instruction and amusement of children) and *Das Frauentranchtenbuch* – whose illustrations were often an open invitation to purchasers to colour, or have coloured, to their own taste. Several of Amman's titles would be reprinted many times, well into the late sixteenth century and again in the mid- to late nineteenth century at the time of the Aesthetic Movement when accurate facsimiles of early woodcut books were made easier by new developments in reproduction methods. Amman's books became popular with the likes of William Morris and other artists in search of inspiration.

Around 1570, in Lyons, another important book was published, *Les Navigations, Peregrinations et Voyages, faicts en la Turquie* by Nicolas de Nicolay, a French geographer-diplomat and quite possibly a spy for Henry II. His book on his travels in Turkey and the Orient, written as he said to promote mutual understanding of other cultures, was hugely popular, published in foreign language editions in Nuremberg in 1572, Venice in 1578 and later in Germany, Holland and England. A

Boluch Baſsi Capitaine de cent Ianiſſaires.

ABOVE & RIGHT Nicolas de Nicolay, *Les Navigations, Peregrinations et Voyages, faicts en la Turquie*, hand-coloured copperplate engraving, 1570

LEFT Johannes de Laet, *Persia sen Regni Persici Status*, woodcut, 1633
RIGHT Wolfgang Kilian, *German Nobleman*, engraving, *c.*1600

large part of its popularity was due to the 60 copperplate engravings depicting Turkish clothing styles, each with an unmistakably fashionable beauty still in evidence over four centuries later.

At this time, clothing styles throughout Europe, as well as throughout the rest of the known world, were localized, regional, typical of a country, a district or even a city. They would remain so until the mid-eighteenth century. The attraction and popularity of this growing genre of publication depended as much on reinforcing regional or national culture and identity as it did on affording readers a look at the differences of others, but in either case cross-pollination of ideas about dress was made possible and popular. At a time when geography was perhaps the most crucial and lucrative of the sciences, so called 'Moral' or 'Cultural Geography' was bound to be of great interest. The tiny (just two-and-a-half by three inches) *Persia sen Regni Persici Status,* for example, by the Dutch son of a textile merchant, Johannes de Laet, was published in 1633 as a prospectus for investors in the new Dutch West India Company – illustrated, tellingly, almost exclusively with woodcut depictions of the exotic dress of the men and women of Persia. Illustrations of the dress of foreigners helped to create some new designs, but more than that, they opened the door to ideas of freedom and choice, both personal and, ultimately, political.

FOEMINA EX PRÆCIPVA NOBI-
litate in vrbe Veneta

Ein Weib auß dem fürnembsten Adel zu Venedig.
Ein herrlich Weib vom Adel/   Wol in der Stadt Venedig/
Geht also her ohn tadel.   Wie die Figur bringt mit sich.
                                          Gg iij

ABOVE & RIGHT Hans Weigel, *Trachtenbuch*, hand-
coloured woodcut, 1577

NOBILIS BVRGVNDVS.

Ein Edelman auß Burgundia.
EIn Burgundischer Edelman/   In solcher klaidung einher tritt/
Wann er vber die Gaß thut gahn.   Wie die Figur anzeigt hiemit.

Aa

Cesare Vecellio, *Habiti Antichi*, woodcut, 1590–98: *Lady of Venice* (LEFT); *Venetian Youth* (RIGHT); *Turkish Courtesan* (FAR RIGHT); *King of the Island of Florida* (BELOW)

In 1577 came Hans Weigel's much admired woodcut book, *Trachtenbuch*. Like Jost Amman, he was a disciple of Dürer, as indeed were the illustrators of the Landsknecht publications. *Trachtenbuch* was published in Nuremberg, again by Sigmund Feyerabend, with 219 single-page woodcut illustrations in full quarto format. It was popular at the time, many taking up the author's invitation to owners to customize their copy by investing in 'the splendour of hand-colouring' and it was reprinted several times, but it lacked the essential appeal of the new or different. That was left to the Venetian artist Cesare Vecellio and his book *De gli Habiti Antichi et Moderni di Diverse Parti del Mondo*, also known as Vecellio's *Habiti Antichi*.

Cesare Vecellio was born around 1522 in northern Italy into a family of artists, the most famous being his older cousin Tiziano Vecellio or Titian as he is now known. As was the custom in sixteenth-century Italy, he began an apprenticeship when he was around six years old and as soon as he had gained enough experience he began to work in Titian's studio in Venice, living with the master's family. By his early twenties, Vecellio had become one of Titian's trusted assistants, working with him on his various commissions and travelling with him to meet prestigious clients, including the Holy Roman Emperor, Charles V, and Philip II of Spain. He made several trips to Germany, where he met and worked with the master woodcutter and engraver Christoph Krieger. He collected drawings and prints of clothing styles during all of his travels, some from other artists and some from Titian, in addition to his own sketches, eventually assembling more than enough for his masterwork.

ABOVE Cesare Vecellio, *Noblewoman of Bologna*

from *Habiti Antichi*, woodcut, 1590–98

Nobile di Borgogna

ABOVE Cesare Vecellio, *A Nobleman from Burgundy*
from *Habiti Antichi*, woodcut, 1590–98

This book contained 420 single-page illustrations, masterfully engraved on wood by his German associate, Christoph Krieger, yet another follower of Dürer. In addition to featuring the popular dress styles of Venice in decorative, as well as informative, illustrations with detailed text, included were peasant costumes from Danzig, the dress of a noblewoman from Bohemia and England, the court dress of nobles from France and Spain, a Venetian courtesan in her finest gown and the beribboned clothing of a German aristocrat. Vecellio travelled and recorded all over Europe, including Turkey, Greece and several Eastern European countries, often contrasting the new styles against the more traditional modes of dress, all of them with a descriptive text in Italian and Latin. It was a virtual feast of ideas for the growing number of tailors and dress-makers who were beginning to be employed, as never before, throughout much of Europe. The second revised edition of *Habiti Antichi*, published in 1598, had even more to offer – 500 illustrations, an extra 80 plates, featuring the dress styles from the newly discovered lands and previously unused images of dress from Asia and Africa.

Now, tailors and dress-makers, as well as painters and artisans, for whom the book was originally intended, had enough to work from, in decorative detailing and cut and style of the various designs, for the rest of their careers. Put simply, these two publications from the last decade of the sixteenth century irrevocably changed the world of European fashion and fashion illustration for the next two hundred years, with Vecellio bringing to flower the seeds sown by Albrecht Dürer a hundred or so years earlier. *Habiti Antichi* was widely sold throughout Europe, where it spread the inspiration contained in its 500 illustrations – the plates were full of usable ideas and they, in particular, began the long path towards the acceptance of an international mix and match style of dressing. Even today, the influence of ethnic detailing, introduced by Vecellio, still plays a major role in the creation of new fashions.

By 1664, literacy had increased throughout much of Europe. A growing fashionable elite and a large number of attendant tailors and dress-makers and their suppliers could read and study the work of Vecellio and others. Many of these quoted from new translations of ancient Roman and Greek texts informing readers that changeable dress styles were not sins against their Creator, as many prelates preached, nor a rebellion against the Church as various popes had determined. These writings, by poets and thinkers like Pliny, Juvenal, Ovid and Martial, long predated the rule of the Roman Catholic Church, and spoke of the then common belief that clothing was one of humanity's important attributes, and that each member of society

RIGHT Giacomo Franco, *Habiti delle Donne Venetiane*, woodcut, *c.*1591–9

was behoven to dress as attractively as possible. In fact, many of the ancient texts posited the idea that dress, like dance and poetry, was an essential part of our humanness. Vecellio's book was an added inspiration to those wanting to enjoy their wealth and add to their sense of self, beauty, comfort and luxury. His books detailed everything minutely and unashamedly – the fabrics, textures, colours, trimmings and accessories, intended as it was, as a source book for the painters of the period.

During his time as an apprentice, Vecellio came to realize that like all other artisans, painters needed help and inspiration in their work, especially with the painting of portraits. To that end, he put as much information as possible into his original text and wrote and published further books of reference, notably his work on the expensive, handmade lace that was becoming such a mark of fashionable dress and wealth. The book, *Corona della Nobili et Virtuose Donne* was published in 1591 in four volumes and, like his other books, was subsequently reprinted several times during the

Persen

Claude-Louis Desrais, after Jacques Grasset de Saint-Sauveur, *Costumes Civils Actuels de Tous les Peuples Connus*, hand-coloured engraving, eighteenth century: *Persian Costume* (LEFT); *Man from Minorca* (ABOVE); *Girl from Lipperotte* (ABOVE MIDDLE) ABOVE RIGHT *Costume from the Urals* from *Bildliche Darstellung aller bekannten Völker*, hand-coloured engraving, eighteenth century

seventeenth century, its influence extending even into the eighteenth century and beyond.

Vecellio observed that in Italy in the sixteenth century, 'clothing as a subject allowed for no absolute certainty, for styles of dress are constantly changing according to the wishes and desires of their wearer.' He appreciated how important and inspirational even the most ordinary ethnic clothing styles were going to be, then and in the future. In his discourse on the evolution of dress and fashion, he noted the use of colourful feathers used by the indigenous peoples of the New World, writing that in their 'extremely beautiful, well-woven garments, divided into sections of feathers of different birds, skilfully and artfully made in such a variety of well-matching colours, that for this reason and for their rarity, they can be considered the most delicate and sumptuous clothing to be found anywhere.' Clearly, and perhaps unusually for his time, he was not an ethnocentric European, but an enthusiastic supporter of newly discovered and existing diversity – a man who helped Europeans realize and define themselves through dress in new and different ways.

Vecellio's books on lace contributed greatly to these changes, having been published just as the use of handmade lace as an important fashion statement was beginning. His illustrations of lace designs were to be minutely copied in many of the painted portraits of the period. This was a time when lace of the finest quality was worth more than its weight in gold and elaborate portraits were in huge demand from artists like Velázquez, van Dyck, Frans Hals, Rubens and many others. It is clear from close inspection of their portraits

Danseuse de l'Isle O-tahiti.

Claude-Louis Desrais, after Jacques Grasset de Saint-Sauveur, *Costumes Civils Actuels de Tous les Peuples Connus*, hand-coloured engraving, eighteenth century: *Taihitian Dancer* (ABOVE); *Taihitian Costume* (RIGHT)

Otaiti portant des présent au Roi.

LEFT Claude-Louis Desrais, after Jacques Grasset de Saint-Sauveur, *Turkish Lady Smoking* from *Costumes Civils Actuels de Tous les Peuples Connus*, hand-coloured engraving, eighteenth century
RIGHT *Costume of Turkish Guards* from *Bildliche Darstellung aller bekannten Völker*, hand-coloured engraving, eighteenth century

that they or, more probably, their assistants and apprentices spent many hours painting decorative lace sections whilst working from samples and source books like Vecellio's.

What is also clear from the portraits painted during the seventeenth and eighteenth centuries is that the artisan painters and their assistants were also being co-opted into the realm of fashion design, using a variation on the 'self-advertising' methods of the young Abrecht Dürer, whose self-portraits – carefully styled, designed and very fashion-conscious – built his reputation and client list. Other painters followed his example, dressing up to impress clients, painting portraits of non-existent subjects wearing fashionable and expensive imaginary clothing. The artist created clothes that showcased their ability to paint fine lace, fabulous jewellery and other trimmings and rich fabrics, all beautifully depicted in glowing oil colours on canvas. These 'dream dresses' and 'dream portraits' were often pure invention – the artist-inventors becoming true fashion designers.

Cah: 16.

Nº 1.

CHAPTER TWO
A TIME OF REVOLUTION

During the seventeenth and early eighteenth centuries fashion itself suffered a great deal through the horrors of religious faction fighting in many parts of Europe and the various edicts of condemnation against sartorial and other freedoms issuing from the pulpit and the Pope. These restrictions resulted in the printing of revised editions of books like Vecellio's *Habiti Antichi*. Artists were using these as a source of inspiration, creating 'dream portraits' of sitters in imaginary fashions to showcase their skill. There was, however, little in the way of new printed fashion material of aesthetic merit until, by the mid-eighteenth century, a new mood of independence from outdated authority was, once again, beginning to be felt. During this turbulent period, England was busily developing new technologies, increasing production of all manner of goods and building a strong export market for its products. The rise of Science and Reason, as guiding principles, spread across the Continent, taking on different national flavours and ideals, ultimately leading to revolution – for some technological, for others violent.

In France, folders and collections of fashion plates were popular, particularly of the nobility, but it wasn't until 1771 that a new genre of publication, with a regular fashion emphasis, was introduced in England. The *Lady's Magazine*, published monthly, was aimed at the growing number of fashionable and educated women of the new wealthier classes. It included a single full-page illustration of a simple dress. In Spain, a revised, hand-coloured version of Vecellio's *Habiti Antichi* was published as a guide to elite, continental dressing.

LEFT The Bonnart brothers, *Personnages de Qualité*, engraving, later hand-coloured, 1680–1715

ABOVE & RIGHT **The Bonnart brothers,** *Personnages de Qualité*, **engraving, later hand-coloured, 1680–1715**

Englænder.

Habillement des Gentilshommes Anglois en 1735. 1745. 1755.   *30.*

LEFT English lady of quality of the 1640s, hand-coloured German engraving, eighteenth century

ABOVE French courtier of the 1680s, hand-coloured German engraving, eighteenth century

ABOVE RIGHT English gentleman of quality of the mid-1700s, hand-coloured German engraving, eighteenth century

Amazingly, Vecellio's publication had stood the test of time since its original printing. By now, however, fashion and the fashionable had other sources of inspiration derived from new forms of commerce and a new source of wealth. For centuries, trade with the East had paid for the elaborate, exclusive lifestyles depicted by the likes of Vecellio and the portrait painters of the Renaissance through to those of the early eighteenth century – rich with expensive lace, and silks and brocades from the Orient. Now, wealth would flow from new home-grown industries, albeit produced from raw materials gathered or swapped for slaves in the colonies. The Industrial Revolution had begun, setting in motion the tireless, seemingly endless money-spinning of 'mass production' and the enormous social upheavals created in its wake.

In the world of fashion, the first visible manifestation of change and rebellion in France surfaced in the late 1770s. Paradoxically, the change came from Marie Antoinette herself, when she initiated a new, liberating summer style that had first been championed by the English fashion illustration of 1771. This illustration showed the simpler dress style worn by an 'English lady of quality' whilst relaxing

ABOVE LEFT *Lady's Magazine*, hand-coloured copperplate engraving, 1789

ABOVE RIGHT First English fashion plate, *Lady's Magazine*, hand-coloured copperplate engraving, 1771

RIGHT Jean-Michel Moreau le Jeune, *Les Adieux* from *Monument du Costume*, hand-coloured copperplate engraving, 1777

Dessiné par J. M. Moreau le jeune.   et Gravé par de Launay le jeune en 1777

LEFT & RIGHT François-Louis-Joseph Watteau, *La Galerie des Modes*, hand-coloured copperplate engraving, 1782 OVERLEAF François-Louis-Joseph Watteau, *La Galerie des Modes*, hand-coloured copperplate engraving, 1782 (LEFT); Pierre-Thomas Leclerc, *La Galerie des Modes*, hand-coloured copperplate engraving, 1778 (RIGHT)

on her country estate. Court life in England was significantly less restrictive than in France and many ladies spent much of their time in the country, where they dressed more casually to accommodate their informal lifestyle. This style became known as 'Le Style Anglais'. In this regard, the French queen was an Anglophile. As a reaction to the strictly codified and hugely expensive costumes required for state occasions, Marie Antoinette set a fashion for soft, English-style dress while relaxing at her country retreats at Marly and the Petit Trianon in attire that many of the court's most influential courtiers considered to be little more than negligées. Made from soft muslin, this dress flowed from the shoulder and was worn loosely belted. The Gaulle, or 'Chemise à la Reine' as it was called, caused outrage in France, especially when the queen commissioned her favourite portraitist, Elisabeth Vigée Le Brun, to paint her wearing the new simple style.

At court, however, Marie Antoinette was extravagant in her mode of dress, encouraged by the court milliner, Rose Bertin, who became the queen's couturiere and the centre of much controversy. She quickly came to be known as the 'Minister of Fashion' – an unofficial title bestowed on her by an angry Minister of Finance. The fashions created by Bertin were extravagant and costly, but far more expensive was the queen's taste in jewellery and her love of ostentatious hats, adorned with the rarest of imported feathers. To be fair to the queen, it must be noted that this love of conspicuous wealth and adornment had become rather the norm among those nobles and their sycophants who made up the court of Versailles and the social elite of Paris. Dr A. S. Rapport wrote in his book on Rose Bertin, *The Creator of Fashion in the Court of Marie Antoinette*,

of the astonishing changes that took place in Paris, beginning at the time of Louis XV's death in 1774: 'A love of luxury was filling Paris and the towns of France with valets, drapers, jewellers, goldsmiths, looking-glass makers, perfumers, wig-makers, tailors, milliners, traders in exotic feathers and expensive fabrics . . . fashion-mongers of all sorts.' This was being 'carried into the rural districts of France and beyond – bringing forth a luxury of initiation which seems to have become, throughout Europe, the fashion.'

By 1778, the fashionable French painters Claude-Louis Desrais, Pierre-Thomas Leclerc and François-Louis-Joseph Watteau, grandson of the famous court painter of the seventeenth century, had been commissioned to create the fashion illustrations for *La Galerie des Modes* or, to give this most beautiful of fashion publications its full English name, *The Gallery of French Fashion and Costumes, drawn from life and engraved by the most celebrated artists of this genre and hand-coloured with the greatest care by Madame Le Beau*. Like the English fashion illustrations of 1771, *La Galerie's* illustrations were printed from finely made copperplate engravings, created by skilled artisans from the original drawings, and then carefully, and beautifully, hand-coloured. The first part of *La Galerie des Modes* was published in Paris by the print merchants Esnault and Raspilly, two printers from Normandy, licensed by the king to publish and print on fashion-related themes. *La Galerie* appeared irregularly, in some 70 portfolios over the ten-year period between 1778 and 1787. Each portfolio contained five or six engravings – near complete sets are rare, so the total number of prints is not exactly known.

ABOVE Pierre-Thomas Leclerc, *La Galerie des Modes*, hand-coloured copperplate engraving, 1778
RIGHT François-Louis-Joseph Watteau, *La Galerie des Modes*, hand-coloured copperplate engraving, 1782

Watteau del.   Duprin sc.

La brillante Lise piquée de l'infidélité que son amant lui a faite, court exécuter un projet de vengeance pour le faire
revenir à elle : elle est coeffée d'un chapeau à la Caravanne, robe a l'Anglaise garnie à la Figaro.

ABOVE LEFT Claude-Louis Desrais, *La Galerie des Modes*, hand-coloured copperplate engraving, 1778

ABOVE RIGHT François-Louis-Joseph Watteau, *La Galerie des Modes*, hand-coloured copperplate engraving, 1787

RIGHT Claude-Louis Desrais, *La Galerie des Modes*, hand-coloured copperplate engraving, 1779

LEFT Claude-Louis Desrais, *La Galerie des Modes*, hand-coloured copperplate engraving, 1778

At first, as if in protest against the archaic rules that inhibited change in dress styles, particularly at Versailles, the talented and intuitive illustrators Desrais, Watteau and Leclerc placed a great deal of emphasis on the feminine hats and elaborate hairstyles, which were powdered and peppered with jewellery, trinkets, exotic feathers and novelties of all kinds. The reluctance of the administration to accept any kind of change to the established court dress codes prevented the normal ebb and flow evolution of fashion, which caused great resentment. The king and his administration, however, remained unaware of the dangers of such denial – in matters of dress or, indeed, anything else. What these beautiful illustrations began to reveal was the shifting of fashion leadership from the court of Versailles to the men and women of Paris – a parallel to the changing political mood of the country.

During the next ten years, an additional 340 illustrations were published in the *La Galerie des Modes*, combining the talents of Desrais, Watteau, Leclerc and Augustin de Saint-Aubin – and the master engravers of the copper plates, Pierre-Julien Dupin, Pierre-Adrien Le Beau, Jean-Baptiste Patas and Etienne-Claude Voysard. Seen by these illustrators, French women's dresses, from 1780 onwards, appear to have become overtly sensual. Men's costume had also begun to adopt some of the English style, including ideas from the dress of the 'Macaronis' – a group of young dandies who, after spending time in Italy in the 1770s, formed a club in London where they would wear brightly coloured waistcoats, breeches, hose and jackets, some with bold patterns, some with zebra stripes and even leopard spots. In France, only a small measure of the Macaroni style was adopted, but the English country style of riding coat, 'le Redingote', and other items became quite the thing 'à l'Anglaise'.

'Le Style Anglais' quickly became fashionable in other capital cities, transmitted with the tacit help and suggestion of the artists of the *Galerie des Modes* and other publications, like the *Lady's Magazine*. The fashion launched, women were soon scrambling, with the aid of their dress-makers, to redesign their next gown, simpler in construction, stripped of heavy decoration – a style that was now devoid of the cumbersome decoration and restrictive back pleat of the *robe à la Francaise* so beloved by the traditionalists.

The *Galerie* illustrators next conspired to get rid of the traditional hip paniers that had been worn at ceremonial court functions for generations, replacing it with a grand court dress with exaggerated back interest known as the 'tournure' – a kind of expensive bustle, which caught the Gallic imagination for a time. Soon, they were featuring illustrations that took inspiration from operas, theatrical

ABOVE Claude-Louis Desrais, *La Galerie des Modes*, hand-coloured copperplate engraving, 1776–8

RIGHT Pierre-Thomas Leclerc, *La Galerie des Modes*, hand-coloured copperplate engraving, 1782

le Clerc Inv.

Bacquoy Sculp.

Robe en Foureau à queue simple, les manches retroußées, la Robe sans garnitures, Fichue -
.Mantelet. Cette Femme est Coëffée d'un Chapeau à la Malbouroug orné d'un frisé de Gaze et de
quelques Fleurs.

ABOVE & RIGHT François-Louis-Joseph Watteau, *La Galerie des Modes*, hand-coloured copperplate engraving, 1780

productions, paintings and illustrated books. Novelty, rather than fashion, took centre stage for the wives, daughters and paramours of courtiers, the ideas spreading out into the salons of the merchant classes. These changes were beautifully illustrated by Desrais, Watteau and Leclerc. Only Augustin de Saint-Aubin seemed to prefer illustrating the more traditional styles worn at court and by actresses and dancers in their most ornate productions.

In 1785, a rival fashion publication was launched in Paris with a different take on the current fashion impasse. *Le Cabinet des Modes ou Les Modes Nouvelles* was a less expensive and more compact publication, but with a wider distribution and a strong audience in the growing merchant class, the bourgeoisie, both in France and abroad. The publishers wisely featured children's and menswear in its finely engraved, delicately hand-coloured copperplate illustrations, and also included the latest word in carriages, furniture and other changing fashion items. As the great Art Deco publisher, Lucien Vogel, would later write: 'The very first fashion magazine, as we know it, was *Le Cabinet des Modes*, founded in 1785 by Lebrun-Tossa, which the following year became the *Magasin des Modes Nouvelles*. It included engravings after Desrais and Defraine, philosophical articles, anecdotes, literary works, comparisons between French and English fashions, articles on jewellery and furniture. To judge by its imitators, its success was immediate. Copies were pirated in Weimar and Liege

ABOVE & RIGHT *Le Cabinet des Modes ou Les Modes Nouvelles*, hand-coloured copperplate engraving, 1785–6

and similar journals appeared in London, Florence, Leipzig, Harlem and Prague. The whole of Europe became interested in fashion.' Lebrun-Tossa, in true Enlightenment spirit, predicted lasting peace as a result of shared taste: 'We were seeking,' he declared, 'to give birth to that harmony, that air of uniformity that many of our French philosophers have been desirous of establishing between all nations of the Earth and we believed that by having them adopt the same clothes, we could eventually have them adopt the same manners, the same customs, even perhaps the same language.' Unfortunately, events would soon take a less peaceful turn.

That same year, the first German fashion periodical was published, the *Journal de Moden*. A smaller publication than *Le Cabinet*, it was aimed at a less cosmopolitan market, but it did broaden its range of illustrative interest. The first issue contained five hand-coloured copperplate engravings on hats, hairstyles, a fashionable chair, decorative room heater, men's riding boots and gloves, elevated women's shoes and one fashionable fur-trimmed winter coat complete

ABOVE Claude-Louis Desrais, *La Galerie des Modes*, hand-coloured copperplate engraving, 1785–6
RIGHT *Journal des Luxus und der Moden*, hand-coloured copperplate engraving, 1787

with muff. It was a magazine obviously intended for a more rural clientele than any previously published, deliberately more English in style and content – more *Lady's Magazine* than *La Galerie*. The new mix was successful in attracting readers, so much so that the the following year, when *Le Cabinet des Modes* became *Magasin des Modes Nouvelles*, they added the words 'françaises et anglaises', acknowledging the growing English influence on the fashions of Paris and the lucrative importance of their British readership. *Magasin des Modes Nouvelles* employed many of the same illustrators for their fashion plates, the best being those by Watteau and Desrais.

In 1787, the *Journal de Moden* also had a name change, becoming the *Journal des Luxus und der Moden*. The proprietor was Friedrich Justin Bertuch, who at the time was described as Weimar's most famous citizen after Goethe. A follower of the German Enlightenment, he was above all a practical man who saw a strong economy, locally based, as the foundation of a happy and healthy society – a stark contrast to the path the French Enlightenment was taking. He was responsible for setting up various industries, including print works, and helped to found an art school in Weimar to educate young artists and designers to ensure the future creation of aesthetic local products. The magazine, published monthly in its distinctive orange wrapper, covered fashions in everything from hats to gardens, carriages to art – anything that might generate a market for German produced luxury goods. In this it was successful but its influence was more significant in educating middle class taste, helping subscribers, with thier growing incomes, to construct an identity for themselves built on aesthetic principles. For anybody paying attention, these two fashion publications showed precisely and clearly the differences between

LEFT & RIGHT **Early Dutch fashion magazine** *Kabinet van Mode en Smaak*, **hand-coloured copperplate engraving, 1791–3**

LEFT & RIGHT *Journal des Luxus und der Moden,* hand-coloured copperplate engraving, 1792–5

LEFT *Journal des Luxus und der Moden*, hand-coloured copperplate engraving, 1792–5

the hard-edged rationality of French Enlightenment thinking and the more pragmatic, human-oriented ideas of the Germans.

Popular at the time was *Costumes Civils Actuels de Tous les Peuples Connus* (Costumes of all the Known Peoples of the World), co-authored by a French-Canadian diplomat and illustrator, Jacques Grasset de Saint-Sauveur, and a utopian-minded journalist, Sylvain Maréchal. It appeared in 158 separate part-issues between 1786 and 1788 and contained 300 hand-coloured engraved illustrations, many by Grasset himself, some redrawn by Desrais, depicting 'the costumes and dress styles that were currently being worn in Europe, Asia, Africa, America and the islands recently discovered by Captain Cook on his recent voyages in the Pacific Ocean'. It was a publication that caught the imagination of the public, particularly those influenced by the new philosophical ideas on the basic goodness and nobility of so-called 'savage' peoples. Its store of illustrative material would influence a new wave of interest in indigenous clothing from around the world. As a result of the public interest in other cultures, as strong in the 1780s as it had been two hundred years earlier, several similar books came on the market, including a similar Weimar monthly, *Bildliche Darstellung Aller Bekannten Volker*.

Although the social, economic and political causes of the dissatisfaction in France are a matter of history, what the fashion illustrations and their accompanying text began to reveal was the shift of leadership from the sycophants of the court of Versailles and its obviously bankrupt autocracy to the growing number of Paris merchants, bankers and businessmen of all types, together with the complicity of their wives, daughters and mistresses. Of the Revolution itself, much has been written, with details of events succeeding events with lightning speed, the Revolutionary Tribunal turning its venom upon itself and the violence of 'The Terror'. Nevertheless, fashion of a kind continued to develop in Paris, Vienna and London, sparsely illustrated as befitted the sparse new fashions. For a time, from 1790 to 1793, the sequel to *Magasin des Modes Nouvelles* continued as *Journal de la Mode et du Goût*; in London, the *Lady's Magazine* was still being published, but with very few fashion illustrations of interest, whilst in Strasbourg, Berlin, Leipzig, Florence and Vienna, new publications containing fashion illustrations began their careers.

The German magazine, *Journal des Luxus und der Moden*, grew in strength and influence and in 1793, its publisher, Friedrich Justin Bertuch, published a manifesto, which gave as his aim the awakening of an awareness in the German people of their own artistic prowess and the wish to instill in German artists and craftsmen more faith in their own artistic powers. His aims, in line with German Enlightenment thinking of the day, were practical. By recommending the luxuries and fashions of Germany to an international readership, the journal would help power the national economy to protect against the dangers and errors which were ravaging France. 'Foppish fashions or manners' would not be encouraged, 'as there is always the danger of damaging excess and dissipation'.

These sentiments were echoed in several other magazines of the period, particularly the large-scale, beautifully illustrated but short-lived *Gallery of Fashion*, which began in April 1794. Like *La Galerie des Modes*, it is regarded as one of the most beautiful of all the hand-coloured fashion magazines of its period. It was created by Nikolaus Wilhelm von Heideloff, a native of Stuttgart, who fled Paris in 1790, where he had been an engraver and painter of fashionable miniatures. In London, he worked for a time with another German, Saxony-born Rudolph Ackermann, one of London's most successful booksellers and a publisher of fine prints, who would later become the publisher of the highly successful *Ackermann's Repository of the Arts*. The introduction to *Gallery of Fashion* stated that the publisher 'will make it his particular study to select only the latest designs of those dresses in which ladies of fashion appear at the routs, the opera, the play-houses and the concert rooms; as well as those elegant morning dresses for Hyde Park and Kensington Gardens', adding that ladies of rank 'will

BELOW LEFT & RIGHT Nikolaus Wilhelm von Heideloff, *Gallery of Fashion*, hand-coloured aquatint, 1794–8

always find the publisher ready to represent their dresses in that style of elegance and that of original taste, which is so peculiar to the British ladies'. Published monthly, each issue contained three, four or sometimes five full-length figures of ladies in two finely engraved and coloured plates, many of which were highlighted with touches of gold and silver, some with added miniature jewellery. These illustrations are particularly notable for their fine backgrounds and incidental details. The list of subscribers was published at the back of each yearly volume of twelve issues, and the names and titles on this list make it very clear that at this time fashion as promoted in Heideloff's *Gallery of Fashion* was only intended for the wealthy elite. As a magazine, it determined to disregard everything that was happening in France, as if problems not mentioned did not exist.

The French Revolution proved to be a turning point for European fashion – it took clothing styles back to classical republican basics. Almost as if they had known that dramatic change was imminent, the illustrators of *La Galerie des Modes* did two things – they captured the ornate styles of Versailles, preserving a little of the ambiance of those last years before the storm broke, and they spotted and charted the beginnings of a fashion for freer, less stultifying clothes, which, in hindsight, surely pointed to a desire for other freedoms. In 1797, as soon as the restrictions on dress were lifted in France, *Le Journal des Dames et des Modes* began its long reign. On a more modest

(738)

Chapeau orné de Rubans de Taffetas. Fichu à pointes nouées en Écharpe.

LEFT *Le Journal des Dames et des Modes*, hand-coloured
copperplate engraving, 1806
ABOVE *Le Journal des Dames et des Modes*, hand-coloured
copperplate engraving, 1799

scale than Heideloff's *Gallery*, but with a much larger audience, its excellent 'Costumes Parisiens' fashion illustrations quickly helped make this magazine an international success and spawned similar style journals across Europe. One such was *Fashions of London and Paris*, published in London by R. Phillips, which often used Paris-made or inspired illustrations. It was through these popular fashion periodicals, and others published in England, Germany, Holland, Italy and Spain, that the new Paris fashions were promoted to an ever increasing international audience. From this time on, Paris would be inextricably linked to fashion and style in the public perception.

With the *ancien régime* gone, simplicity reigned. By 1796, fashionable dress for women had been reduced from a tightly corseted, one-and-a-half-metre-wide carapace to an unstructured slip of fine muslin, which looked as if it had been draped directly onto the naked female body. Known as the 'Grecian Style', decried by many as the 'Naked Style', it was popularized by the elegant Josephine and her

ABOVE LEFT & RIGHT *Le Journal des Dames et des Modes*, hand-coloured copperplate engraving, 1801; 1806
RIGHT *Le Journal des Dames et des Modes*, hand-coloured copperplate engraving, 1812

emulators, the 'Merveilleuses', and would become the silhouette of post-revolutionary France and, indeed, most of Europe. In 1798, the influential *Lady's Magazine*, now including fashion illustrations in every issue, published its first illustration of this new French 'naked' fashion. The editor also ran a complaint, written by a member of the French National Institute, attributing the blame to the collections of 'improper' Greek statuary that had been used to decorate public parks during the Revolution: 'It cannot be doubted that the current immodesty of our women can in part be attributed to the immodesty of our statues. The women punish us for our contempt of decency, by assuming a similar clothing, the thinness and transparency of which leaves no longer anything to be desired with regard to the discovery of concealed charms.' By 1800, this transparent trend had spread across the Channel, as reported and illustrated in another English fashion magazine, the *Lady's Monthly Museum*, which began publishing in 1798. The journal editors, responding to negative reactions, defended the new fashion styles and their duty to print what they saw as

Costume Parisien.

Negligé Boiteux.

Bonnet de fantaisie.

Robe à la
Demi-Psyche.

Bonnet du Matin.

Mise Ordinaire.

newsworthy – the 'Naked Style' was after all boosting their readership figures. They described in detail the draping of the diaphanous muslin dresses, what jewellery should be worn, who made the best slip-on shoes, which style of coiffure to adopt, what form of underclothing, if any, should be worn, what cosmetics to use and how, with one journal even tackling the subject of trimming and decorating pubic hair. Others satirized and caricatured the Merveilleuses as self-indulgent and ridiculous, happily adding to the polemic.

Soon there were angry letters of complaint. One such letter came from a mother of four, who said that the new French fashion 'has turned the heads of my unfortunate daughters. I hear nothing now, but Grecian drapery and the frippery of foreign absurdity ... they now expose their person in a style of dress absolutely indecent.' Another called this fashion 'one of the most lascivious styles ever worn by civilised people'. Two months later, the same magazine published the 'Papal Bull Against Female Dress', in which the Pope ordered that these new fashions 'should be repressed by fine or corporal punishment' and that these punishments should be extended to 'all such damsels, who at first sight may appear properly attired, but are nevertheless decked in transparent robes' and also to those who 'display themselves seductively'. There were reports of an actress being forced to leave the stage of a Drury Lane theatre when the audience 'threw their handkerchiefs on to the stage so that she might dress herself properly'. A letter from a man who had travelled in North Africa and the Middle East drew the readers' attention to a copy of the pre-revolutionary

H.B.2.H.   No:1

book *Costumes Civils Actuels de Tous les Peuples Connus*, which, he said, was incomplete but nevertheless did show that the European ways of dressing were not the only ways of adorning the human body. The uproar about this new fashion continued for months, one assumes to the great delight of the publishers. It was clear that there was a very real market for this kind of publication – the fashion magazine, as we now know it, had established itself.

At the beginning of the nineteenth century, a new breed of fashion designer and illustrator began to emerge, encouraged in France by Pierre de La Mésangère, proprietor of the long-running *Le Journal des Dames et des Modes*, with a German version being published out of Frankfurt. Both editions featured the new Grecian styles from Paris, and the slightly more ornate versions being worn in London. It was La Mésangère's influence that spread this new style throughout Europe, marking out Paris once again as the most important fashion centre of Europe. His lead was followed by such publications as *Fashions of London and Paris*, *Lady's Monthly Museum*, *Le Mois*, *Le Miroir de la Mode*, *Magazin des neuesten Französischen und Englischen Geschmacks in Kleidungen* and many others, published in

LEFT *Magazin des neuesten Französischen und Englischen Geschmacks in Kleidungen*, hand-coloured copperplate engraving, 1798

BELOW *Modes et Manières du Jour*, hand-coloured copperplate engraving, 1798

Munich, Vienna, Berlin, Florence, Leipzig, Milan, Nuremberg as well as London, Paris and Frankfurt – with the majority of the illustrations originating in, or at least influenced by, Paris. This was the period when Paris fashions were said to change from week to week with 'such delicate shades of change, that it is almost impossible to distinguish between them'.

By 1806, *La Belle Assemblée or Bell's Court and Fashionable Magazine* began in London, with each monthly issue containing two very beautifully engraved fashion plates. Several of the illustrations, although not credited, appear to be the work of a young Henry Moses, who would soon begin work with Thomas Hope on his influential *Costumes of the Ancients* – two fully illustrated volumes published in 1810, which was to greatly influence English interior and furniture design and English, French and European fashions for many years to come. Moses also drew for the *Lady's Magazine*, which, in 1807, featured the Greek furnishings and dress details he was by then preparing for Thomas Hope. These, together with Lord Elgin's Greek acquisitions, Napoleon's excursion into Egypt, the new Etruscan and Pompeian discoveries, sparked a wave of neoclassicism in everything from dress to architecture. The initial reaction to the Grecian dress may have been shock and outrage, but it was largely adopted, with regional variations, as being more natural, practical and almost

ABOVE *Neuste Moden der Kleider und Meubles aus London*, hand-coloured copperplate engraving, 1793

RIGHT *La Belle Assemblée*, hand-coloured stipple-engraved aquatint, 1809

Printed for the LL.ᵗʰ Number of La Belle Assemblee, Published by John Bell, May. 1.1809.

Cheltenham Summer Dress.

ABOVE & RIGHT *La Belle Assemblée,* hand-coloured

stipple-engraved aquatint, 1810

classless, with a return to the influences of the Renaissance and the adoption of rich colour combinations of the Old Masters.

Many of the new fashion journals and periodicals contained interesting illustrations of these new 'democratic' styles, some featuring the latest fashion for imported cashmere shawls, ideal for wearing over flimsy muslin. But there were also the beginnings of a more formal dressing style encouraged by Napoleon, who in 1804 proclaimed himself emperor and began to reintroduce all the trappings of a royal court. Napoleon wished his court to be the most splendid in all of Europe, in part to re-establish the position of French luxury goods in the marketplace. To this end Napoleon was known to rebuke ladies who attended his splendid receptions and balls for the 'sin of economy' – being dressed in something he had seen them in before was an unforgiveable faux pas. Younger women became the centre of attention and attraction, dressed in Athenian style, gowns made from expensive diaphanous fabric, breasts pushed up and on full display. The scantiness of many of the dresses of this period were beautifully captured by the illustrators, as were the later, more demure styles that came into fashion between 1810 and 1820.

In general, menswear and male aesthetics fared somewhat differently from those of women, particularly during the late 1790s, after the killing times had run their course. In France, the Incroyables – the male equivalent of the Merveilleuses – became, for a brief time, the dandies of their day, sporting a kind of uniform – enormous lawn cravat that often engulfed the chin, 'guillotine victim' hairstyles which were long at the front and sides, shorn at the back, imitating the way prisoners were prepared for the blade, earrings, exaggerated pointed shirt collars and long jackets with wide, colourful lapels often spelling out their allegiances and political leanings. Their influence faded once Napoleon took command and male fashions quickly became unified. A combination of factors – war followed by the enormous growth generated by the Industrial Revolution and the extra responsibility placed upon men of wealth and influence, particularly in England, by expanding world trade – began to totally change their lives and their look.

Those men of wealth who became bankers, merchants and manufacturers required a specific style of dress – nothing that too closely resembled the aristocratic garb of pre-revolutionary days, but with a definite, though understated, stamp of authority and wealth. They chose an adaptation of the army uniform that had already made its mark on male fashion – a style introduced by leading Savile Row tailors in London, its lines drawn from the uniforms worn by Napoleon and Wellington. Professor J. C. Flügel, author of *The*

Psychology of Clothes from 1930, claimed that this change from the ornate and sumptuous aristocratic mode of satin knee breeches, embroidered waistcoats, silk stockings and high-heeled, silver-buckled shoes, amounted to the male abandoning his claim to be considered beautiful; henceforth his only aim was to be useful, the recognized bread winner and provider, correctly and appropriately attired, rather than beautiful, elegant or modish.

By 1812, while still living under the continuing threat of war and possible revolution, most wealthy men had begun to dress as discreetly as possible, almost anonymously, adopting a look which was transformed from military beginnings to become a dark, three-piece business suit. Apart from shortening the jacket and the introduction of pinstriped trousers around 1820, this suit was to remain virtually unchanged until very recent times. The truly fashionable man might take discretion to new heights and expensive reserve to the level of art, by becoming a follower of George 'Beau' Brummell, whose philosophy turned around his belief that a gentleman should never be noticed for what he wears. Except for the way he ties his cravat and wears the finest, freshly laundered linen, a man should never be ostentatious, must look at ease in his garments which, although of the highest possible quality, should never appear to be new. To that end, it is said, he had his new suits 'broken in' by his valet. He believed that a gentleman should distinguish himself by small details, so discreet and often so expensive as to be unnoticeable and unattainable by the average man, but of sufficient interest to attract the attention of those in the know. Eventually, Brummell's style would prevail over the fops and Macaronis in setting the standard for menswear, though both were linked in a new fashion for masquerade balls and costume parties, disliked and preached against by the ecclesiastics and moralists. These events gave the participants a chance to break the rules – wear the dress of 'pagan peoples' or figures from history, and many women preferred to dress as men. A report in a London magazine at the end of the eighteenth century stated that 'many ladies of rank and beauty chose to adopt the male mode of dress for the evening and appeared as masculine as many of the delicate "Maccarony" things we now see swarming everywhere in London, to the disgrace of our noble, patient British race,' but it continued, 'they looked lovely and charming and were justly admired.'

CHAPTER THREE
ILLUSTRATIONS FOR ALL

With the restoration of the French court by Louis XVIII, after Napoleon's defeat and final exile to St Helena in 1815, French fashion and French fashion illustrations once again began to blossom with renewed vigour. To quote French fashion historian Octave Uzanne, 'the continually changing dresses of this period are a never-ending delight to the artistic eye. Gazing at them, we seem to hear the silken rustle of the delicately clinging, softly trimmed garments and feel the charm and overmastering fascination wielded by the now free and fearless beauties, whose fair forms peopled this new, exciting age of freedom.'

The presence of English, Polish and Russian troops during the reinstatement of the monarchy brought a new palette and array of finery and detail into vogue, and when international trade picked up, the new Paris fashion magazines and their news-hungry editors were not slow in taking advantage of these trends, quickly adding more illustrations to their periodicals. The fashion plates concentrated more on trimmings and details in female dress, while menswear was focused on the symbols that could elevate the basic form of utilitarian dress that had evolved since the Revolution. The cut and fit of the jackets and the trousers, for example, hinted at the owning of horses and an ability to ride – one of the chief attributes of a man of property and position. Such small, subtle details became important in menswear. Often the fashionable change was so discreet that only those with the current knowledge could discern the difference.

In 1806, the London entrepreneur publisher John Bell started his beautifully illustrated *La Belle Assemblée* in London, which was followed by *Ackermann's Repository of Arts* in 1809. Both of these very British publications included some fine fashion engravings but few

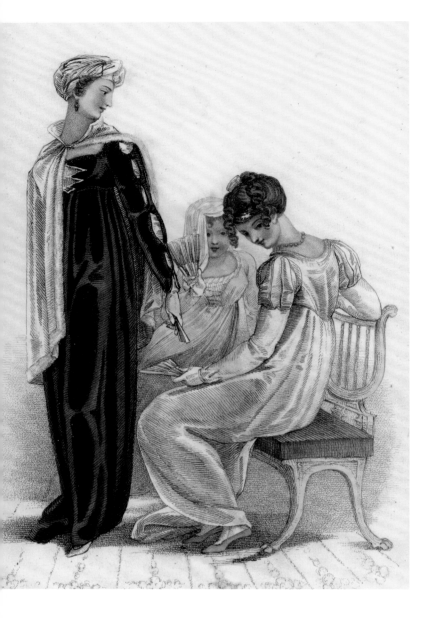

were signed. The world of fashion illustration became a different proposition – almost a battleground between the competing editors, publishers and the all-important fashion illustrators and only the best fashion magazines and journals were destined to survive. Among the survivors was the long titled *Lady's Monthly Museum, or Polite Repository of Amusement and Instruction: Being an assemblage of whatever can tend to please the fancy, interest the mind or exalt the character of the British fair* – a fashion journal edited by a 'society of English ladies'. Then there was the *Corriere delle Dame* out of Milan, while in Germany, the *Zeitung für die elegante Welt* began in Leipzig and the *Journal des Luxus und der Moden* continued, the only fashion magazine to predate the Revolution, still regularly featuring hand-coloured fashion plates and keeping to its original manifesto.

The publisher of the *Journal des Luxus,* Friedrich Justin Bertuch, was keenly aware of the growing influence of English fashions, saying in one issue that the 'tasteful simplicity and solidity which

MORNING DRESS.

England alone has known how to bestow on its fashionable products is so extraordinarily commendable and enticing, that the very word "English" already has an irresistible enchantment'. Knowing this and wishing to free Germany of all outside fashion influences, he began to publish only Weimar fashion illustrations, designed, engraved and printed by local artists, which he believed would increase demand for the styles featured. This he hoped would increase local production of fashionable merchandise, increase the population's confidence in their own aesthetic and free them from the influence of the French and the English. He believed that this would invigorate Weimar's industry and economy, spreading prosperity and increasing the chances for a decent livelihood among his own people. It was a system that had worked well, even during the devastation wreaked by the Napoleonic Wars.

Bertuch's vision of increased productivity within a country, aided by the use of locally produced fashion illustrations and fashionable

ABOVE *Corriere delle Dame,* hand-coloured
copperplate engraving, *c.*1820
RIGHT Philipp von Stubenrauch, *Wiener Zeitschrift für
Kunst, Literatur, Theater und Mode,* hand-coloured
copperplate engraving, *c.*1820

P. v. St. del.

Fr. Stöber sc.

XXX. *Wiener Moden.* 90. 1820.

ABOVE Philipp von Stubenrauch, *Wiener Zeitschrift für Kunst, Literatur, Theater und Mode*, hand-coloured copperplate engraving, *c.*1815

ABOVE Philipp von Stubenrauch, *Wiener Zeitschrift für Kunst, Literatur, Theater und Mode*, hand-coloured copperplate engraving, *c.*1820

merchandise, also worked well in England, when both *La Belle Assem-blée* and *Ackermann's Repository of Arts* helped the British dress trade during the embargo on trade with France during Napoleon's time. Ackermann included fabric swatches from English fabric merchants on specially illustrated pages, along with well-illustrated fashions designed to inspire ideas for the fabric's use. His periodical included pages of advertisements for ready-to-wear clothes for the new season, available at various London shops. To further mark their difference from the French magazines, both *La Belle Assemblée* and the *Repository of Arts* were larger than their French competitors.

By 1820, all the industries connected to fashion had developed to a point unimaginable in the 1790s, with British-made textiles now selling worldwide. The *Repository of Arts* also began to include furniture, interior designs and romanticized domestic architectural designs in its monthly publications. Reliable postal services were becoming a feature of life, increasing the spread and number of subscribers to periodicals, and there is evidence that from 1810 both English and French fashion journals were being imported into New York and elsewhere in the Americas – increasing as transport and mail systems became more established. In the gossip columns of many of these journals there are a number of references and letters to and from America but, despite various attempts to produce a truly American fashion publication, none succeeded until 1828,

BELOW *Les Modistes* from *Le Bon Genre*, 1932 pochoir reprint by Jean Saudé of the 1827 original hand-coloured engraving
RIGHT *La Belle Assemblée*, hand-coloured stipple-engraved aquatint, 1809

Concert Room Full Dress   Nov. 1. 1809.

Engraven for La Belle Assemblee N52. Publd by J Bell Proprietor of the
Weekly Messenger Southampton Street Strand December 1 1809

when the first monthly copy of *Godey's Lady's Book* was published in Philadelphia.

Between 1797 and 1820, the *Journal des Dames* published more fashion images than all the other fashion magazines combined, but by 1820, the average purchaser of the journals was changing. The new readers, most of them already wearing the current styles, wanted to see future fashions. The new *Petit Courrier des Dames*, published out of Paris, was, with its beautifully drawn hand-coloured illustrations, the best weekly fashion journal of that period, with every sixth or seventh illustration being of menswear and every fourth or fifth being of well-illustrated fashionable hats. Between the first issue in 1822 to the end of the 1830s, it published 1,602 well-drawn, hand-coloured fashion plates. As with the *Journal des Dames*, which appeared every

BELOW & FAR RIGHT *Le Journal des Dames et des Modes,* hand-coloured copperplate engraving, 1812
RIGHT *Le Journal des Dames et des Modes,* hand-coloured copperplate engraving, 1815

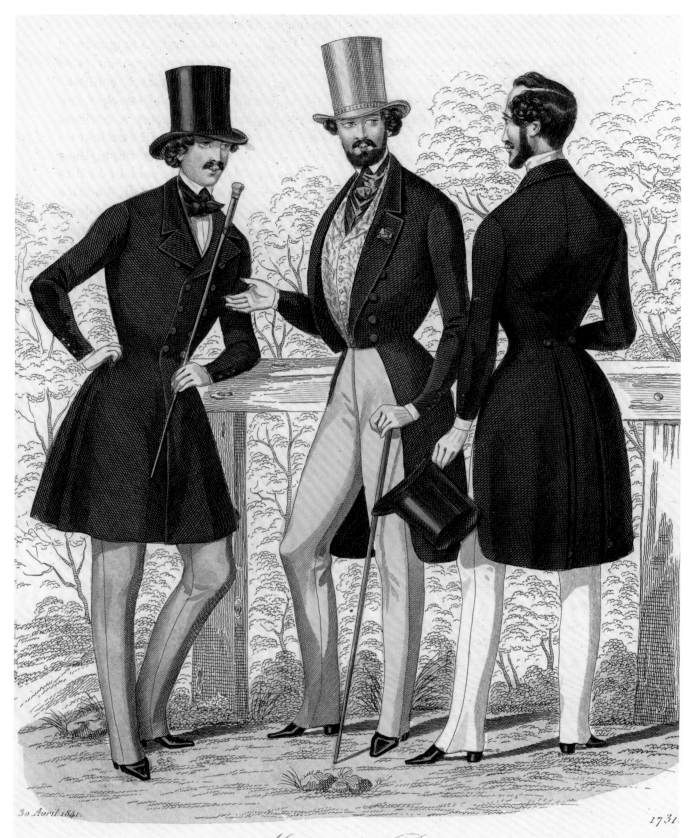

3o Avril 1841.   1731

Modes de Paris.

Petit Courrier des Dames.

Boulevart des Italiens, N.º 2, près le passage de l'Opéra.

Modes de Longchamps.

LEFT *Petit Courrier des Dames*, hand-coloured steel
engraving, *c.*1841
ABOVE *Petit Courrier des Dames*, hand-coloured copperplate
engraving, 1820s

Erstes Extrakupfer.

five days and always with a very attractive fashion illustration, the *Petit Courrier* was designed and printed in a compact size, conducive to easy postage, further ensuring an ever widening readership.

In 1826, maintaining its high standards to the end, the Weimar monthly *Journal des Luxus und der Moden* published its last issue – its pre-revolutionary mandate was no longer viable or necessary. Foreign travel and trade was on the increase and those wealthy enough to travel wished to show evidence of this sophisticated, status-enhancing activity in their clothing. Paris became the central crossroads of all fashionable travel in Europe. With this influx of potential customers, the luxury goods ateliers of the capital flourished. Thanks to this boom and the growing expertise of the fashion illustrators who captured it, many of whom had grown up with images such as those in the *Journal des Dames*, Paris was well on its way to becoming the centre of future fashions.

Originally it had been possible for each new fashion publication to design and print their own illustrations from local engravings. But great skill is needed for a really well-engraved fashion plate, and by the mid-1820s, with its ever increasing use of intricate, decorative detailing, it was clear that this was an art in which the many Paris ateliers excelled. Paris, in fact, was best placed – geographically,

ABOVE German menswear, hand-coloured steel engraving, *c.*1840
RIGHT *Petit Courrier des Dames*, hand-coloured steel engraving, 1841

25 Janvier 1841.   1705

Modes de Paris.
Petit Courrier des Dames.

Boulevart des Italiens, N° 2, près le passage de l'Opéra.

Robe en tulle façon de M.me Leroy, r. S.t Honoré, 332. Fleurs de Chagot. Travestissement.
de Babin. Gants Mayer. Eventail Duvelleroy. Sous-Jupe crinoline. Chemise de Doucet rue
de la Paix.

Mess. S. & J. Fuller, 34, Rathbone Pl. Lond.

ABOVE & RIGHT *Petit Courrier des Dames*, hand-
coloured copperplate engraving, 1820s–1830s

culturally, aesthetically, historically – with the skills needed to cater for the growing interest in and need for changing fashions. Soon most of the illustrations used in European periodicals and magazines began to originate in Paris. Even the newly published *Graham's American Monthly Magazine* used Paris-drawn plates, re-engraved locally, as did the first few issues of *Godey's Lady's Book* in 1830.

In European cities, the changeover from locally produced fashion illustrations to those created in Paris was phased over a period of several issues, with the French ateliers adding the magazine's name to the top of the plate. Within a matter of months, however, most foreign publishers were asking the French suppliers to add the words 'The latest Paris fashions', in a variety of languages, to their fashion-plate orders – some eventually requesting all the text to be in French, regardless of their destined country of publication, since it added a touch of Gallic chic that impressed their readers. Once Paris had firmly established itself as the production centre for the supply of hand-coloured fashion illustrations, some of the ateliers began to specialize in high-quality work for the more prestigious publications, while

ABOVE LEFT *World of Fashion*, hand-coloured copperplate engraving, 1830

ABOVE *Petit Courrier des Dames*, hand-coloured copperplate engraving, 1820s

RIGHT *Townsend's Monthly Selection of Parisian Costumes*, hand-coloured copperplate engraving, *c*.1830

267

1. Chapeau de Paille orné de fleurs, Robe de foulard, Canezou en tulle brodé.

2. Capote de crèpe, Robe de foulard, Pèlerine en tulle brodé.

LEFT & RIGHT *Petit Courrier des Dames*, hand-coloured steel engraving, 1854

others were reorganized for quantity, rather than quality, production, with print runs of a single illustration often being in excess of 10,000 and occasionally up to 25,000. These larger print runs were no longer individually coloured by specialists. Instead, teams of colourists were employed and paid per hundred prints coloured. By the mid-1830s this had led to a general lowering of the illustrative standards among the cheaper publications such as the *Ladies Penny Gazette*, which started in 1833 and which has its place in our collection not for aesthetic merits but as evidence of the widespread appeal, through all strata of society, of fashion illustration.

The majority of the fashion illustrations in this and earlier chapters were printed from finely made copperplate line engravings, with carefully detailed shading, created with fine parallel lines or stipple dots or a mixture of the two. Although the skill of the engraver was

of the utmost importance, skill alone was not enough to produce an aesthetically pleasing print. The magic of a good fashion print was the result of the successful combination of an engraver's skill and the imagination of the artist. Quality print runs, which with hand-printing methods were limited, usually to fewer than 5,000 copies, could now, with new machinery, be increased to 100,000. For such large runs, mechanized printing presses were needed and developed, the engraving being applied to cylindrical revolving steel plates.

Accompanying this dramatic increase in sales and decrease in prices were short cuts in the printing and colouring of fashion illustrations. This, and the demand for greater novelty of design, led to a marked decrease in the overall quality of the illustrations. At first glance, the public's appetite for novelty and decorative touches added an amusing quality to the illustrations, particularly those between 1825 to 1840, but even then, the illustrators were beginning to run out of ideas. One has to remember that between 1797 and 1839 La Mésangère's *Journal des Dames* alone issued 3,624 different fashion plate illustrations, with new twists needed every five days and every one, for the most part, expected to delight the eye. With that kind of output, however, it is understandable that ideas grew stale and a little repetitive.

Although there was a decline in quality, those designed by Jules David, A. De Tavern, A. M. Adams and Adèle-Anaïs Toudouze and the other ladies of her family are better than most. The quality of hand-colouring of these prints also deteriorated. Those of 1840 to 1880 were coloured by teams of young children, often aged between five and ten. The children worked at long tables in an assembly line, an illustration being passed from one to another, each child applying one colour to one area only, before passing the plate to the next child down the line until it was fully coloured. A crude form of stamped on linocut or stencil colouring was also used for more complicated areas with the final colour being added by the pochoir method – an illustrative and colouring stencil technique that was to reach its height of excellence during the later Art Deco period.

BELOW & RIGHT Jules David, *Englishwoman's Domestic Magazine*, hand-coloured steel engraving, *c.*1860

THE FASHIONS

Expressly designed and prepared for the

Englishwoman's Domestic Magazine.

AUGUST 1860

By the 1830s, few of the fashion magazines were actually illustrating the current fashions, as had been the practice of many of the earliest publications: sheer force of demand for newer and more decorative fashion plates led many of the illustrators to invent designs and details continuously, adding more and more to the basic existing silhouette, ultimately affecting the way people dressed. If one multiplies the total fashion plate output of the *Journal des Dames* by the similar output of at least ten major competitors, it becomes apparent why most of the fashions of this period became so ornate and cumbersome, and why, between 1840 and 1880, women's dresses became so extraordinarily extravagant and intricately detailed, often rivaling the fashions of the fallen court of Versailles. This is not to say that all the fashions and fashion illustrations produced during this period should be disregarded: they are an accurate reflection of the changes taking place in society and many have charm, if little aesthetic merit.

During the years between 1840 and 1860, in an attempt to cope with the increasing demand for these ever more ornate fashion illustrations, teams of illustrators and engravers were being employed, each specializing in just one aspect or one part of an illustration. Some did nothing but design or engrave backgrounds, others the faces or hands, the details of a dress or the hats and accessories; others specialized in drawing and engraving children, dogs, embroidery or lace work. Very few came from the hand of one designer-artisan.

Other aspects of fashionable life were changing during this period, to some extent due to the spread of Parisien fashion imagery, which

ABOVE **Jules David,** *Le Conseiller des Dames et des Demoiselles,*
hand-coloured steel engraving, 1852

LE CONSEILLER DES DAMES & DES DEMOISELLES   169, rue Montmartre.   Juin 1853.

Paris, Un an 10 francs   Journal d'économie domestique & de travaux d'aiguille   Province, 12 francs.

ABOVE Adèle-Anaïs Toudouze, *Le Conseiller des Dames et des Demoiselles,* hand-coloured steel engraving, 1853

continually reinforced the message that the best and the latest was to be found only in Paris. The welthy became frequent visitors to the city, as did the fashionable aristocracy of Europe. The French, it seemed, missed certain aspects of royalty and of Napoleon's reign as emperor, with one revolution for the restitution of the Bourbon monarchy, followed by another against. In 1848, a landslide victory returned Prince Louis Napoleon as the new head of state, but by 1852, he was no longer a prince; instead Napoleon III was Emperor of France and by his side was the perfect hostess of the international set and 'face' of French fashion, the beautiful Spanish-born Eugenie – 'the Empress Crinoline'.

Fittingly, for a period defined by technology and industry, even female underwear was 'engineered', introducing enormous, steel-framed petticoats and many outstandingly ugly but fashionable styles. As Octave Uzanne wryly commented, in his book on the history of fashion in Paris, 'with the second empire we reach the most hideous period in female dress that has ever vexed the artistic eye.' London's Great Exhibition of 1851 demonstrated that life was becoming more industrialized and, because of that, social power and prestige moved and spread into the new, wealthier class of merchants, bankers and manufacturers. These rather prudish, self-made men established a style of dress that came to symbolize their new social position. They adopted an adaptation of the earlier three-piece suit, with a three-buttoned jacket in a good quality, black wool, reminiscent of the hunting coats of the gentry, a short waistcoat in a sombre red and proletarian grey striped trousers. It was a utilitarian suit, easily adapted to the individual physique of the newly rich by bespoke tailors, who specialized in hunting attire for the aristocracy and had no problem making these garments. Soon, the discreet three-piece suit became the obligatory mode of dress for all men of standing and it was now women who would bear the responsibility of displaying the family's wealth and social position. It was this display that the fashion illustrators were expected to feature in their work.

To achieve the tiny waist depicted in these illustrations, corsets, made from whalebone and steel, became a necessity. Corsets of a lighter nature had been worn by fashion conscious women in France since around 1805, to push the bosom upwards and to slim the waist, with English and American women of fashion following suit a few years later. By the 1850s and with the aid of the latest technology, the new corset was a truly formidable waistline controller, worn not only by women but by men as well, though few fashion illustrations reveal the underlying garments and gadgetry of this period. Instead, they chose to revel in the glorious excess of fabric, used as the fashionable skirt became larger with the aid of another industrialized invention, the crinoline – a metal and whalebone petticoat that drawings show could have measured up to five metres around the hem with the over-skirt often being heavily trimmed and decorated. By the end of the decade, fashion had reached that point of endless extravagance about which the moralist Jean de La Bruyère had complained nearly two centuries earlier: 'One fashion has scarcely destroyed another, when its turn makes way for that which follows it and this will not be the last; such is our fickleness.'

The popularity of the American magazines – *Godey's Ladies Book*, *Monitor of Fashion*, *Ladies Gazette of Fashion* and the numerous imported titles – created an urge to travel in those rich enough to do so, whilst others stayed home content to write letters, complaining and commenting unfavourably on the new European fashions as seen in imported fashion illustrations. The author of one such letter in *Godey's Ladies Book* observed that 'whilst the French ladies are using cosmetics to aid their beauty, the ladies of England are once again wearing low-necked dresses which display the full round of their breasts.' American

RIGHT 'Travestissement' in *Petit Courrier des Dames*, hand-coloured steel engraving, 1850s

ladies, however, 'fired with Puritan spirit, have reacted strongly against both of these trends and devised a fashion of their own to gain attention of members of the opposite sex and the envy of members of their own'. They tilted their crinoline skirts to display their ankles, sewing lace edging around their underdrawers and petticoats. The display of the ankles, and gradually more and more leg, and a glimpse of the forbidden undergarments, became a characteristic of American fashions in the latter part of the nineteenth century – a tendency that was destined to take over future fashionable trends – even though this practice and the bifurcated undergarments they were beginning to wear were denounced by numerous ecclesiastics and moralists.

Fashion may have been fickle at the time, but fashion magazines or periodicals aimed at women were far from being merely simple or silly. Literacy was on the increase, as was the education of working

1. Juli 1852.

Beilage zur allgemeinen Musterzeitung.

class children of both sexes, driven in part by the frequent demands published in the various fashion journals and magazines. Women's political rights were often featured and there was also a growing appetite from female readers for news and debate as much as fiction and poetry.

By this stage, many of the inheritors of wealth began to reject the prudence of their forefathers, whose sober attire had symbolized dignified allegiance to a bank or boardroom, in favour of a style that made no apologies for a privileged position. Others began to dress according to convictions, like the women influenced by Amelia

1. Juni 1853.
Beilage zur allgemeinen Musterzeitung.

1. Mai 1853.
Beilage zur allgemeinen Musterzeitung

LEFT *Allgemeinen Musterzeitung*, hand-coloured steel
engraving, 1852
ABOVE *Allgemeinen Musterzeitung*, hand-coloured
steel engraving, 1853

Bloomer, an advocate of dress reform that included less restrictive fashions for women, or the men and women who dressed to mirror their interest in artistic 'bohemian' pursuits. Some journals of the period complained about the 'ambitious and unfeminine members of the fair sex who have, in their struggle for power, contended for the wearing of those articles which formerly characterised the male costume' and deplored those young men who adopted the 'pouting-pigeon bodices of the females . . . today's "dandy" is now so bolstered up in collars and frills, so lost in baggy trousers, so pinched in the middle by whalebone stays, that he can neither have an expansion of heart nor fair use of limb.'

Such moralizing editorials were common in the mid-nineteenth century, a reaction no doubt to the speed at which times were changing and perhaps to the hypocrisies and contradictions that were becoming apparent. In Britain, Victoria and Albert were the models of respectable family life, while in the French court stories of excess and debauchery were rife. The Industrial Revolution was in full swing and wealth was increasing for many, while for others, particularly in the big city slums, life became increasingly difficult, almost unlivable, even though goods of all kind were cheaper and more plentiful than ever before, for those with the means to enjoy them. Progress and technological development, as was proved in the hugely successful Great Exhibition of 1851, touched every area of life. Printing, publishing and photography were developing rapidly; the Suez Canal opened, making the world seem smaller, as did the introduction of train travel and steel-hulled ships; scientific discoveries and ideas like Charles Darwin's evolutionary theories were causing anger and debate; and on the fashion front, the invention of the domestic sewing machine, and cut-to-measure paper patterns in the latest styles, the introduction of the crinoline and then the metal cage that supported the bustle were changing the shape of women and fashion illustrations of this period.

In 1867, a new fashion magazine was published in New York. *Harper's Bazaar* (or *Bazar*, as it was then) cost 10 cents for eight pages of text, profusely illustrated with black and white illustrations. It was published by agreement with the German *Der Bazar*, which started in Berlin in 1854. It was primarily aimed at the American middle class. Unlike its competitors, such as Frank Leslie's *Gazette of Fashion*, which featured illustrations redrawn from French and English periodicals a year or more after their initial appearance, *Harper's Bazaar* made arrangements for several of the leading European magazines to provide fashion illustrations in advance of their own publication. 'Our readers will thus be sure of obtaining the genuine Paris fashions, simultaneously with Parisians themselves.' Fashions worn in New York, 'which may be styled the Paris of America', were also featured, as were advertisements for expensive European fabrics and the like. Today, *Harper's Bazaar* has a unique record. Not only was it the first weekly fashion journal to be published in the USA, but in 1970, with the demise of the British *Queen* magazine, *Harper's Bazaar* became the world's oldest surviving fashion publication.

Queen magazine began in 1861 as *The Queen: The Lady's Newspaper and Court Chronicle*, with eight pages of text and line illustrations of points of fashionable interest. At the end of each month, a hand-coloured litho, folio-sized fashion illustration, printed in France, was issued, featuring the very latest styles. Also in 1861, a new Bavarian weekly fashion magazine, *Münchener Bilderbogen*, was published. Each weekly edition contained a supplement of *Zur Geschichte der Kostüme* (the History of Costume) – four groups of figures dressed in colourful historical, regional and national costumes. These plates were immediately successful, since it was known that the great Charles Frederick Worth himself drew on historical, artistic sources for inspiration. The series continued well into the 1880s – over 1,250 sheets of vivid chromolithographic colour, in excess of 10,000 individual figures – a mine of design ideas from different historical times and cultures, the illustrative style evolving over the years of the series' publication. The colourful litho prints of the 1860s presented the regional dress of Spain or imagined the kimonos of the ancient Japanese, the courtly style of Elizabeth I and Louis XII, men in

SUPPLEMENT — The Queen THE LADY'S NEWSPAPER AND COURT CHRONICLE — DECEMBER 4th 1875.

Imp. Gilquin Paris.

LATEST PARIS FASHIONS

Presented to the subscribers to the Queen. The Lady's Newspaper and court chronicle.

LEFT Isabelle Toudouze, *The Queen: The Lady's Newspaper and Court Chronicle*, hand-coloured lithoprint, 1875
RIGHT Adèle-Anaïs Toudouze, *La Mode Illustrée*, hand-coloured steel engraving, 1877

fashionable lederhosen with magnificent decorative detailing. Later came chromolitho plates focusing on vanished civilizations depicting the dress of Phoenicians, Egyptians, Assyrians, Celts, Romans and others in exquisite detail and in glowing colour, a bonanza of references and ideas that began to influence and seep into artistic minds who twenty years later would become the fashion illustrators and designers of their generation. The series would spark many rivals. One of them was the beautifully put together *Le Costume Historique* by Albert Racinet, produced by Firmin-Didot in France, who incidently also revived interest in Cesare Vecellio's work with yet another popular reprint.

Another of the new inventions of the period to catch public attention was photography. By the middle of the nineteenth century, numerous daguerreotype studios had sprung up in the major cities specializing in portraits, and it became quite the thing to have one's exact image captured onto a glass plate. By 1865, newer methods made it possible to make multiple prints on to paper to send to friends and family. Exciting though it was to see one's exact likeness, ladies soon realized that a crinoline, while charming in a fashion drawing, was not exactly flattering seen in a photograph. Before the decade was out, it would be replaced by the bustle, another metal contraption, but one that pulled and draped the skirt fabric to the back, creating a slimmer silhouette which was far more photogenic than the crinoline. One aspect of the bustle, which must not be forgotten, was its importance as a conspicuous display of wealth to enable the rich to keep one step ahead of the new, growing middle class. It was vital to use masses of fabric in a dress – any less would be interpreted as a loss of prestige. The bustle provided a new and necessary means of support for this display, and it became the focal point of most of the fashion illustrations of the period.

1867 was the year that many American businessmen came to Paris for the first time – some to visit the new French International Exhibition, some accompanied by their wives and daughters, who returned home with trunkfuls of 'French treasures', enthralled by the style and excitement of a glittering court and its attendant high society. Just three years later, however, French fashion was to receive a terrible jolt and lose much of its new American patronage, when the Franco-Prussian War put an end to the Second Empire. Without the splendour of the court of Napoleon III and the Empress Eugénie to admire, fashion turned to the theatre for its inspiration and in the process became increasingly eclectic. Women of fashion began appearing in costumes that might have come straight from plays set in Renaissance Italy, others in dresses that could have been designed by van Dyck – the influence of *Zur Geschichte der Kostüme* and Racinet's *Le Costume Historique* was everywhere. Other gowns looked like elaborate confectionary, 'like mounds of spun sugar candy', lavishly trimmed with artificial flowers, ribbons, braids and passementerie work of beads and sequins. It seemed the question was no longer how to dress well, but how to dress as extravagantly as possible. Other fashion commentators, including the likes of Baudelaire, noted that 'although some women were like sheep as they followed each other in matters of dress – flounces were in fashion, everyone, whether thin or tall or short or fat, appeared in flounces – the present fashion seems, however, to be showing us more or less everything under the sun, as ladies decorate themselves, each after their own idea.'

Amid all of this, there was one fashion, or rather fashion aid, that continued to hold both European and American women in thrall – the corset, despite criticism describing it as 'barbarous'. The fashionable look in the late 1860s was to be 'much flounced and puffed, with chignons, high heels and waists so tightly laced that their shoulders are made quite square', emphasizing their décolletage and, of course, the back interest of the bustle – all shown in the fashion illustrations of the period by such artists as Héloïse Leloir, Adèle-Anaïs Toudouze and her mother and daughter, Alexandre-Marie Colin and Isabelle Toudouze, Paul Gavarni, Laure Noël, Jules David, François-Claudius Compte-Calix, Gustave Janet and Louis-Marie Lanté. The fact that these artists were named was also something of a milestone in the developing business of commercial illustration. The customers for Paris fashion plates were now becoming more discerning, allowing the best of the illustrators and engravers to step out of the obscurity in which most commercial artists of the day worked, and build a name for themselves.

The 1860s was an era of great change for Parisian fashion. Traditionally, most wealthy women took a published fashion plate to their dress-maker and had it copied or adapted to their needs, or in the larger dress-making establishments they may have been able to try on one or two ready-made dress styles and have them tailored to fit. With the opening of the couture house of Worth and its competitors, this traditional way of dressing began to change. Worth attracted a large and lucrative clientele, drawn mainly by his designs for the Empress Eugénie. By the mid-1860s, the House of Worth was dressing the crème de la crème of international society – royalty, the aristocracy, as well as a number of those wealthy Americans who had flocked to the great Paris Exhibition. Other outlets, like the increasingly luxurious department stores, were attracting customers with their selections of ready-made clothing and accessories, furnishings and objets d'art and advertising was becoming a bigger feature of every fashion periodical.

As more of France's factories began to be mechanized and fabric became cheaper, competition in the dress trade became fierce. To boost sales and increase productivity, the emperor encouraged what Uzanne called 'the fashion for fashion', insisting on greater and greater luxury at court, with the trickle down effect ensuring that, very quickly, new style garments were within the reach of the average citizen, at least in the capital. Fashion in France, Britain and elsewhere was no longer restricted to the upper and middle classes, with the English author Robert Smith Surtees noting, 'This speedy influx of fashion and abundance of cheap and tawdry finery has well nigh destroyed the primitive simplicity of country churches. The housemaid now dresses better – and at all events – than her mistress did twenty years ago, and it is almost impossible to recognise working people in their Sunday dresses.'

CHAPTER FOUR
THE FERMENT OF CHANGE

For France, 1870 was a fateful year that brought unrest, war and the end of the Second Empire. The production of fashion illustrations, upon which so many foreign publications relied, became difficult and patchy. Only adaptations of the illustrations from the German magazine *Die Modenvelt* were available to publishers in London and New York, under the title *The Seasons* – a popular, multi-language magazine which had a wide distribution throughout Europe. In the hiatus, perennial favourite *Zur Geschichte der Kostüme* proved to be a treasure trove of ideas for retro-fashions and costumes, as masquerade balls and 'travestissement' – fancy dress – became popular forms of entertainment. Eventually, the series was published in two volumes and was followed in France by Augustin Challamel's history, *Fashion in France from Gallo-Roman Times*, beautifully illustrated, printed and coloured in gouache, using the latest pochoir stencil-based printing techniques.

In that pivotal year, the French were defeated by the Prussians and Paris was beseiged. For a time the Paris Commune took control and the House of Worth, only the year before the largest and most successful of the couture houses, was taken over as a hospital and all of his rivals were closed. The ateliers that produced most of the French fashion plates for home and overseas customers were closed until 1872, while the brilliant, fashion-conscious court of Napoleon III and his consort, Eugénie, became just a memory. For a time, Paris lost its influence over the wider fashion scene and in the lull Europeans began to experiment with retro, as well as oriental, themes and ideas. Some were searching to create an essentially timeless, 'aesthetic'

RIGHT 'Travestissement' in *La Mode*, hand-coloured steel engraving, 1850s

Journal des Demoiselles
Modes de Paris. Rue Drouot. 2

mode of dressing, like the British Pre-Raphaelites and the designers and artists of the Arts and Crafts movement: William Morris, Walter Crane, Jessie M. King, Archibald Knox and Rex Silver. This mix would became the hallmark of the new and fashionable London emporium Liberty, which promoted a mix of Tudor, Celtic and oriental influences, quickly named 'Style Liberty' – a tribute to Mr Liberty's encouragement and support of the development of Art Nouveau in Britain.

As with all periods of great social, cultural and commercial change, there was reaction, quickly visible in fashion and picked up on by the popular publications. The accepted styles of fashion illustration disappeared. New editions were generally larger in size – a trend started by the English weekly *The Queen: The Lady's Newspaper and Court Chronicle* as early as 1861, when the preferred

ABOVE LEFT 'Travestissement' in *Journal des Demoiselles*, hand-coloured steel engraving, 1880s
ABOVE RIGHT 'Travestissement' in *Le Journal des Modes*, hand-coloured steel engraving, 1880s

female shape was still tightly corseted and crinolined. By the mid-1870s, the monthly hand-coloured folio-sized litho fashion plates were showing a distinctly different female form. It has been fairly well documented that women appear to change their shape in agreement with newly emerging fashions. Degas complained about this change in 1878, saying that the feminine sloping shoulders, once de rigueur, with the delicate decolletage of the crinolined evening dresses, had disappeared. He considered the new focus on broader shoulders to be a sign of decadence.

The change in emphasis on the part of many of the newer fashion illustrators was created by the arrival in Paris of many of the daughters of newly rich American bankers and barons of industry, owners of fast-growing railways and shipping magnates. These young ladies

LEFT V. Huchot, *Les Modes d'Enfance,*
hand-coloured steel engraving, 1873
RIGHT *Journal des Demoiselles*, hand-
coloured steel engraving, 1880

were marrying into European and British nobility, bringing with them new blood, hefty dowries and a very different upbringing and outlook. The later fashion drawings of Charles Dana Gibson and the colourful illustrations of Harrison Fisher epitomize these girls, showing them as tall, healthy, active and decisive. These were young women used to sporting activities and a degree of freedom not common in European society. They were generally taller, with longer limbs and broader shoulders than most European girls. It was this young American female that many of the new illustrators and designers now set out to woo and capture in their work.

By the mid-1870s, these young Americans were regular visitors to London and Paris and were having a great influence on the collections that the Paris couturiers were beginning to show each season. It was these fashions that the illustrators of the new, more commercially minded magazines, like *L'Art et la Mode*, *Le Petit Echo de la Mode* and *Le Salon de la Mode*, started to feature, with an emphasis on colour, particularly pastel shades. Illustrations of menswear of this period,

Mame et Falconer imp Paris

LEFT & ABOVE *Le Journal des Modes*, hand-coloured steel
engraving, 1880s

329

ADMINISTRATION DES JOURNAUX DE MODES

25. Rue de Lille. Paris

Parfumerie-Oriza de L. Legrand, f. des Cours de Russie & d'Italie. 207.r. S. Honoré.-Foulards & Cachemires de
l'Inde pour Costumes. Malle des Indes. 26. Pg. Verdeau.-Robes & Manteaux de M.me Laurence Hardy. 76. r. de Rivoli.
Bijoux de fantaisie de la M.on Senet. 35. r. du 4 Septembre.-Corset Anne d'Autriche & Ceinture-Régente de M.mes de Vertus
12. r. Auber.-Chaussures de M.on Bernier. Laffon. 160. r. Montmartre.-Modes & Chapeaux de M.me Mélice. 8. r. de Richelieu.

by contrast, were restricted to varying shades of brown and black. The established look of the successful industrialist or banker was unchanged, but variations on facial hair were numerous – the clean-shaven young poets of the Romantic era gave way to generations of side-whiskers, moustaches, longer hair and beards – all beautifully depicted in the fashion illustrations of the day.

English men's tailoring techniques began to feature in Parisian women's fashion, with both the couture houses of Redfern and Creed, along with Worth, expanding their business into sporting and outdoor clothes – archery, yachting, croquet, tennis and cycling, all of which required soft tailoring and the invention of knickerbockers. London's fine tailors also received a boost from the American elite, for although their wives and daughters preferred to shop at Worth or some other Paris couturier, the husbands preferred to be outfitted in London – a tradition that continued right up until the Second World War.

In 1878, the Paris International Exhibition opened along the banks of the Seine. It proved to be a great cultural as well as financial success, drawing millions of visitors from all over the world to the French capital. For the industrially minded there was an early form of electric light to wonder at, a wax cylinder that played recorded dance music and a solar energy engine. One of the most visually stunning exhibits featured a display of textiles and artifacts from the recently 'opened' Japanese islands. This new influence was to have a much needed stimulating effect on fashion illustration and creative output of all sorts, including the growing market in children's books and the work of fashion-conscious painters, interior designers and architects. Ever since the Renaissance, Parisian taste has had an insatiable appetite for the exotic, the extraordinary and the fantastic, with their artists, furniture makers, fabric designers and dress-makers being ready to draw inspiration from the Orient, Persia and Arabia. In no other city has fashion and the art of fashion illustration been taken as seriously as in Paris.

The euphoria for change and difference that had been created by the International Exhibition, the steadily expanding international trade and growing wealth of the middle classes created many new avenues for emerging fashion illustrators. Many of these artists saw the difference between western and Japanese dress as equivalent to the difference between sculpture and painting. In Europe the natural body shape was used as the basis for the cut and construction of clothing – the various parts, such as sleeves, collar, bodice and trousers being cut to size and shape, then sewn together to emphasize the three-dimensional shape of the body. But the traditional Japanese costumes, presented at the International Exhibition, showed kimonos made from flat, straight-edged pieces of cloth, woven to size and sewn together, edge-to-edge, resulting in vertical seams that ignored anatomical differences. No form-accentuating devices like corsets or pads were used, resulting in a look very different to that being worn on the streets outside the exhibition pavilions. As a source of inspiration, this new aesthetic flavouring, simpler but with a deep respect for craftsmanship, was to permeate artistic life for the next few decades, eventually giving birth to Art Nouveau. 'Japonisme', as Siegfried 'Samuel' Bing, the father of Art Nouveau in France, would later write, 'had entered the artistic bloodstream'.

The kimono, in its westernized form the peignoir, was already an essential garment in the newly fashionable boudoirs of Paris society – along with new forms of lingerie, silk stockings, laced whalebone corsets and attractively decorated shoes. These more intimate items of a fashionable woman's wardrobe were beginning to be hinted at by the new group of artists and fashion illustrators, who were well aware of their significance to the increasingly influencial *demi-mondaine*s, who had come to prominence in the court of Napoleon III. The illustrators instinctively knew that in fashion, and fashion illustration, there were no rigid rules and that it was their responsibility to challenge out-of-date authority and ways of thinking. They had as examples women like the Comtesse di Castiglione, Cora Pearl and others, the so-called *grandes horizontales*, who, though often 'low-born', used their beauty and wit to rise in society. The thoughts and comments of authors like Dumas, Baudelaire and Uzanne and the keen attention being payed by painters of the day to shopping and fashion (that ultimate consumer marriage) became the stuff of art, raising the bar and opening new vistas for young illustrators entering the field.

Under their dresses, no matter how ambivalent or reserved those outer garments were, fashionable women contrived to be 100 per cent feminine. Along with the still required corset, they wore open, separate-legged pantaloons, pulled together by a draw-string (hence 'drawers'), beautifully embroidered, ribbon-threaded and lace-edged, a lace-trimmed chemise and one or several decorative petticoats. But soon, because of the scandal created by the open-legged pantaloons, worn by the can-can dancers at the Moulin Rouge, the inter-leg seam began to be closed. This was the time when lingerie came into its own, although at first, without the popular press comments, one would hardly know this from the hand-coloured fashion plates. At the same time as critics were condemning the can-can and music hall artistes like Nini la-Belle-en-Cuisse, clerics were threatening damnation to any woman who even contemplated stitching the crotch of her drawers. By the 1890s, however, dancers being drawn to the City of Light with

RIGHT Jules David, *Le Moniteur de la Mode*, hand-coloured steel engraving, 1885

LE MONITEUR DE LA MODE

LA GAZETTE ROSE ILLUSTRÉE, LE BON TON ET L'ÉLÉGANCE PARISIENNE RÉUNIS

Paris, Rue du Quatre-Septembre, N°3.

Toilettes de M.elle TURLE, 9, r. de Clichy — Jupons et Tournures de P. de PLUMENT, r. Vivienne, 33 — Veloutine FAY, r. de la Paix, 9.

Entered at Stationer's Hall

Nr. 21.   Monatlich vier Nummern.   Berlin, 30. Mai 1887.   Preis: Vierteljährlich 2½ Mark.   33. Jahrgang.

Der Bazar.
Illustrirte Damen-Zeitung.

Ueber Kinderanzüge.

Der Inhalt der heutigen Nummer gilt in seiner Hauptsache dem leiblichen Gedeihen der kleinen, eben zum Leben erwachten Menschenknospe und der für das hilflose Wesen sorgend bedachten Mutterhand. Da wir indessen gerade diesem Gegenstande schon wiederholt unsere Aufmerksamkeit gewidmet haben und mit praktischen Rathschlägen den jungen Müttern zur Seite standen, so beschränken wir uns heute auf die betreffenden, in dieser Nummer enthaltenen Abbildungen und Beschreibungen und verweisen — um nicht Gesagtes wiederholen zu müssen — auf die eingehenden Mittheilungen über die „Ausstattung der Neugeborenen." Einrichtung einer Kinderstube" rc. auf Seite 213 des Bogen 1885, und Seite 222 des Bogen 1886. Denn auch die ermachsenen Kinder verlangen von uns ihr Recht und das um so mehr, als für sie der Mode beruht einen gnädigeren und fürsorglicheren Blick erübrigt als für das Kleinste, dem seines weiches Leinen, Flanell und Baumwollenstoffe noch die kostbarsten Güter sind. Sobald es aber beginnt diesen Hüllen zu entwachsen, und die erste entschiedene Neigung zeigt, auf eigenen Füßen zu stehen, streckt auch sofort die Mode die Hand nach dem kleinen Bürger ihres Staates aus, die junge Mutter zwingend, ihren Gesetzen zu folgen. Und wie gern fügt sich diese! Welch ein Triumph leuchtet aus dem zärtlichen Mutterauge, wenn das Kleinod im kurzen Kleidchen, dem Attribut seines ersten Lebensjahres, Gehversuche macht. Das erste Kleidchen ist für Mutter und Kind ein gleich bedeutsames Ereigniß, und mit Sorgfalt und Freude unterzieht sich erstere der Aufgabe, ein solches zu construiren. Es ist nicht ganz leicht für den kleinen Körper, dessen Glieder noch so zart und empfindlich sind, ein recht kindliches und passendes Kleidungsstück zu fertigen. Es soll nicht pressen und drücken, nicht beläftigen oder Gehbewegungen hemmen, denn das kleine Wesen, dem noch die Sprache versagt ist, kann uns nicht mit irgend einer Andeutung unterstützen, und jenes Unbehagen, das sich in Thränen oder Unart kundgiebt, liegt oft an unzweckmäßiger Kleidung. Bis zum zweiten Lebensjahre mindestens dürfte es daher rathsam sein, die Kleinen, gleichviel ob

Knabe oder Mädchen, möglichst lose und bequem zu kleiden, bei nöthiger Gewährung des Schutzes jede übermäßige Erwärmung zu vermeiden und doch von früh an auf eine gewisse Schicklichkeit der Kleidung zu achten. Jede wirklich verständige Mutter wird so viel richtiges Empfinden für ihre Lieblinge haben, daß sie von allen Modethorheiten der Kindertoiletten absieht und aus Rücksicht auf die moralische Entwickelung der Kinder auf

Einfachheit Bedacht nimmt. — Blusen- oder Faltenkleidchen mit Passen sind die geeignetste Art. Kinder von 1—2 Jahren zu kleiden, denn sie erfüllen vollauf die oben erwähnten Bedingungen. Vorlagen dieser Gattung hat der „Bazar" zu jeder Zeit gebracht und solche finden sich auch in der heutigen Nummer (siehe Abb. Nr. 56 und 58). Abgesehen von den hübschen carrirten Wollenstoffen, die in der freundlichen Wirkung der Farben eigens für Kinder erdacht zu sein scheinen, und in dem Wenigen, dessen sie zur Herstellung bedürfen, doch so hübsch und reich an Resultaten sind, erinnern wir an Kleidchen, die der Beihilfe der Handarbeit: wie Stickerei, Häkelarbeit, Strickarbeit rc. unterstellt sind und die am Ende viel zu Geschenken ausersehen werden. Einfarbige Wollen- und Baumwollenstoffe, Frischleinen u. s. w. mit Kreuzstichstickerei, Fischgrätenstichen, point-russe sind immer noch beliebt, und ebenso gern werden kleine Roben in écru, crème oder weiß aus durchbrochener Stickerei hergestellt, die sich über einem farbigen Unterkleidchen von Satin, mit farbiger Schärpe recht stattlich ausnehmen. Neuerdings auch haben sich in Folge des mehr und mehr zunehmenden Wollenregime gerade für Kinder aus Wolle gehäkelte Kleidchen eingebürgert. Dieselben haben viel für sich, denn sie sind elastisch und warm zugleich und schmiegen sich besser der Form des Körpers an als genähte Stoffe, verbürgen also stets ein gutes Sitzen. Und selbst im warmen Sommer wird ein Kind die Wärme dieses gehäkelten Kleidungsstückes nicht als Last empfinden, denn der Charakter der Arbeit erlaubt vollauf den Zugang der frischen Luft, weshalb wir denn aus sanitären Gründen besonders Kleidchen, Unterröckchen, Mäntelchen, Paletots, Jäckchen rc. aus Wolle gehäkelt für kleine Kinder empfehlen. Neuerdings fertigt man auch aus grauem oder crème-farbenem Garn gehäkelte Kleidchen, die an Gediegenheit bei weitem die durchbrochen gestickten Kleidchen übertreffen. Diese waschbaren gehäkelten Kleider bedürfen eines farbigen Unterkleides und veranschaulicht Abb. Nr. 13 auf Seite 143 d. J. ein solches.

Je mehr das Lebensalter vorschreitet, um so größer sind die Anforderungen, welche an die fleißige Hand der

Nr. 1.   Garten- oder Strandhut.
Nr. 3.   Garten- oder Strandhut.   Nr. 2.   Garten- oder Strandhut.
Beschr.: Vorders. d. Schnittmuster-Bogens.   Nr. 4.   Hut für Mädchen.

LEFT Cover art for *Der Bazar*,
woodcut, 1887
ABOVE *Der Bazar*, hand-coloured
steel engraving, 1887

its reputation for naughtiness and newness were prepared to go even further. The Americans Loïe Fuller and Isadora Duncan threw off more than convention in their performances. They danced naked under thin costumes, often no more than a whirl of transparent veil and colourful back-lighting. But, while the dancers and chorus girls were doing their best to push the envelope of propriety, nicely brought up young ladies were being consoled (or bribed) with promises of a trousseau full of the most exquisite lingerie – delicately made lace, ecru silk with softly coloured ribbons, all shown in tasteful black and white on the inside pages of the larger fashion publications like *La Mode Illustrée*, *Les Modes de la Saison*, *Der Bazar* and *The Queen: The Lady's Newspaper and Court Chronicle*.

If the underclothes were fantasy and froth, the taste was for reserved outer garments. As Octave Uzanne made clear in his book, *Fashion in the Nineteenth Century*, when writing on the 1880s and 1890s: 'The most special characteristic of contemporary female dress is the elaboration of undergarments, which, during the last fifteen years, has reached a pitch commensurate, by contrast, with the simplicity and sobriety

LEFT *Der Bazar*, hand-coloured steel engraving, 1887
ABOVE *Der Bazar*, hand-coloured steel engraving, 1890s

of all gowns and outer habilements. This has been the inevitable and legitimate result of the adoption of the English habit of wearing tailor-made clothes out of doors; all the dainty slendours and pretty trumperies which must necessarily enwrap the female form divine, have been driven inwards. Lingeries and stay-makers cannot make their handiwork too exquisitely sumptuous for their fair customers. No lawn can be too fine, no embroidery too cobweb-like, no silk too transparent, no skilfully treated tissue too light, too fleecily soft, too daintily coloured and perishably delicate in colour . . . so prodigious has this branch of feminine fashion grown, that a whole volume might easily be devoted to the subject.'

Throughout the 1880s magazines like *Harper's Bazaar* continued to grow in importance. Reflected in their pages was the growing middle class interest in women's sports, including previously male-dominated activities like fencing and yachting. By 1890, with the new rage for cycling, it at last became acceptable for women to wear a form of trousers in public. Something along the lines of Turkish trousers, long and amply cut, this garment was 'made of such a fullness, that when standing upright, the division between the legs is obliterated', but although some small concessions were made for sports, such as cycling, tennis and croquet, 'a lady of fashion still has to wear her corset and bustle, no matter how strenuous her activity.'

So, while the crinoline morphed into the bustle, the corset remained – although the fashion magazines carried an increasing number of diatribes and theories about the use of tight lacings, not to mention the religious opposition to closing the under-leg seam of ladies' undergarments and the growing use of cosmetics. These publications began to lead the way forward for women, carrying articles on women's education, health, politics and voting. Even in periodicals for young girls, articles encouraging new thinking abounded. There was an increase in the number of special journals for children, with a growing emphasis on physical exercise, particularly for girls, which prepared the way for the new thinking on corsets and clothing. *Every Girl's Annual* of 1883–4, for example, included a series of colour illustrations of young women partaking in gymnastics and other activities as well as regular fashion features aimed at their young readers. In one such article a Japanese inspired fashion illustration, printed in full colour, was included, intended to broaden their young minds and open an aesthetic pathway for the future Art Nouveau style of design. Publishers in the expanding market of children's illustrated books were encouraging their illustrators, like Walter Crane, Richard Doyle, Eleanor Vere Boyle, Kate Greenaway and so many others, to experiment with the new forms of colour

RIGHT *Der Bazar*, hand-coloured steel engraving, 1887

PI-LXXXXIX.

Berlin S.W. 11 Charlottenstrasse.

DER BAZAR,

ILLUSTRIRTE DAMEN-ZEITUNG.

Juli 1887

printing – with their more creative images influencing those of the fashion illustrators.

Orientalism and particularly the work of Japanese printmakers was beginning to change the course of fashion itself. Their influence on fashion, and the closely associated decorative arts, had in fact been growing in importance since the opening of trade with Japan in the mid-1850s, even though many women still preferred the more expensive, ornate European styles. However, the Japanese influence received a boost in 1878 and again in 1889, when unique collections of traditional kimonos, hand-printed silk textiles, samurai armour, ancient ceramics, ukiyo-e prints, lacquer work, netsuke carvings and many other items became the centre of attraction at various exhibitions, including those held in Paris. Work from China, Russia, Persia and Turkey was greatly admired during the 1889 World's Fair, bringing it to the attention of the wider public. Among artists, it had already been an influence on designers like Gallé, van de Velde, Guimard and William Morris, painters such as Monet, Degas, Whistler, Manet and van Gogh, and illustrators such as Mucha, Grasset and Toulouse-Lautrec. The end result was the Art Nouveau style.

The spectacular exhibits at the Paris Exposition Universelle of 1900 were a triumph for the protagonists of the new Art Nouveau design style, which the fashion illustrators, designers and artists had been promoting since the 1880s. In Britain, the 'Style Liberty' was well established and the continental chapter, the Viennese Secessionists, brought their version to new heights, with the buildings of Josef Hoffmann, the paintings of Gustav Klimt and Koloman Moser and later the fashion designs and illustrations of the Wiener Werkstätte, which in turn harked back to some of the core beliefs of the *Journal des Luxus und der Moden* of the 1780s and 1790s. Art Nouveau gave a new, aesthetic unity to design of all kinds, reintroducing natural forms into an increasingly industrialized world. The swirling curves of the new style were everywhere, in architectural details, furniture, jewellery and even the female silhouette, thanks to S-bend corsets used to produce the curvaceous hour-glass silhouette.

As with the previous Paris International Exhibition, the Exposition Universelle of 1900 was built in the very heart of Paris, bordered by the gardens of the Champs Elysées, the Trocadero, the boulevard des Invalides and the Champs de Mars, dominated by Gustave Eiffel's extraordinary steel tower, constructed as the centrepiece of the 1889 World's Fair, which marked the high point of the belle époque. The 1900 exhibition centrepiece, on the Champs de Mars and facing the Eiffel Tower, was the magnificent Palais de l'Electricité, decorated with over 10,000 multicoloured electric lights. The exhibition welcomed visitors from all around the world and was described by one American journal ist as 'a triumph for the protagonists of the Art Nouveau style of design – a celebration of pastel colours, free-flowing forms and curvilinear shapes, created by the French designers', each of whom had utilized the prevailing Japanese influence in an individual way. Their products, it was said, 'reaffirmed French supremacy in the world of European art and design'.

The general theme was one of celebration of the past with a hopeful turning towards the future and the new century. There were striking exhibits by the likes of Charles Lewis Tiffany from New York and Paul Kruger of Berlin, and paintings by artists like Whistler, Degas, Renoir and Sargent. Hundreds of thousands of people from all over the world flocked to Paris to see the work of the twenty-one nations and their colonies participating in the exposition – exhibits from India, Russia, Turkey, China, Persia and other eastern countries. Many of those visitors, while in Paris, made a point of going to see the latest collections created by the famous couturiers of the period – Doucet, Doeuillet, Worth, Paquin, Redfern and the Callot Soeurs – each of whom ran large *maison de couture*. They also visited the forty or so smaller couture houses and the similar numbers of milliners, furriers, jewellers and elite shops specializing in the newly fashionable lingerie and *robes déshabillés*. Since the late 1880s, most of the larger establishments had presented their latest design ideas twice a year, in February and August, when their international clientele came to select their wardrobes – peignoirs, simple dresses for morning visits, outfits for luncheons, clothes for afternoon walks and receiving visitors, and the more sumptuous and ornate dresses for special occasions, official ceremonies, family gatherings, sermons and lectures, artistic receptions, first nights, dinner parties, concerts, visits to the opera or to a ball, not to mention appropriate wear for the races, shooting parties or trips to the seaside. Nothing could be left to chance for the rich and privileged, who studied each new fashion magazine's illustrations with great diligence, searching out the most envy-inspiring styles.

It became fashionable to visit the famous ateliers run by the leading designers and master craftsmen, such as Gallé, Lalique, de Feure, Grasser and Gaillard, who were producing new ideas in glassware, ceramics, tapestries, carpets, silverware, furniture, china, lacquer work, deluxe edition books and *objets d'art*. For others, there were different delights to be found in Paris – on the streets and boulevards, young girls and attractive gigolos plied their trade, while in the specialty *maisons closes*, the madams offered every conceivable variety of pleasure. Moving in more rarefied circles the *demi-mondaines* were the most fashionable of the French courtesans: the elite of their

RIGHT Eugène-Samuel Grasset, *La Grande Dame*, wood engraving and chromotypography, 1896

La Grande Dame

REVUE DE L'ÉLÉGANCE
ET DES ARTS

ADMINISTRATION & RÉDACTION
N° 45 AN⁰⁰ MAISON QUANTIN, RUE S⁺ BENOIT, 7 PARIS

Septembre 1896   PUBLICATION MENSUELLE (4ᵉ année)   Le numéro fr. 50

LES MODES

L. CHALON. — ESSAI D'UN STYLE MODERNE

ABOVE Louis Chalon, *Les Modes*, coloured lithograph, 1901

ABOVE Georges de Feure, *Les Modes*, photogravure, 1902

profession. They exerted great influence over the princes, aristocrats, industrial barons, bankers and millionaires who competed for their favours. Even in the last decade of the nineteenth century, the most famous of these women aroused great interest among the general public, who avidly followed their amours and copied their fashionable styles. They engendered the same interest and admiration that many film stars enjoyed during the golden age of Hollywood and the famous Paris couture houses often used these ladies to promote their fashions, dressing them for little more than cost. There was intense rivalry among these professional beauties, and they and the couturiers exploited the situation in sensational manner. Respectable women of society clamoured for, and avidly copied, the fashionable styles worn by *les horizontales*.

By 1901, many of the leading ladies of the theatre were also used by the couturiers to set new trends, both on stage and off. The styles they wore scandalized, amused and captivated society and their private lives seemed as outrageous as their public lives were glamorous. They acted as fashion models for the new French fashion magazines such as *Les Modes*, an expensive deluxe publication produced entirely by the latest methods of automatic printing on newly developed glossy paper with the first hand-coloured fashion photographs. The magazine was almost twice the size of the most popular fashion-plate magazines of the time. Its first issue included thirty-six monotoned photographs of the very latest Paris fashions, furniture, jewellery and interior schemes, many showing an oriental influence. For the first time, magazine subscribers could actually see how the new twentieth-century styles of design really looked, instead of an artist's interpretation, thus appearing to outdate hand-coloured fashion plates overnight. Readers could now see for themselves the latest influences, in all sorts of new consumer products, and for a time the work of the fashion illustrators entirely disappeared from the pages of the more fashionable magazines. By contrast, many American journals and fashion publications were still happy to employ the skills of illustrators such as Charles Dana Gibson and his beautiful line drawings of Gibson Girls became widely accepted as the ideal American woman.

Thanks to the increasing refinement of the half-tone and line etching process, by 1905 new methods afforded greater freedom in fashion illustration techniques. Soon, by means of a series of extra plates allowing for colour reproduction, there was no longer any reason why artists should be restricted as to the medium they preferred.

It was this freedom from restraint, and the fact that an illustration need no longer be looked upon merely as a fashion drawing, but as a serious work requiring aesthetic skill and creativity, that helped to give distinction and character to the work of fashion illustrators of this period. As the American critic James B. Carrington wrote of the work of Harrison Fisher and the development of colour printing in magazines: 'The privilege of using colour has done more than anything else toward developing the work of the modern illustrator along the broad lines of art.' Harrison Fisher studied illustration at the San Francisco Art Association before working for a local newspaper. He became a regular contributor to the leading American journals and periodicals, largely responsible for the success of the *Saturday Evening Post*. He illustrated the fashionable, well-groomed young American woman, depicting her, as Carrington put it, 'refreshingly free from self-consciousness and there is never the least suggestion of the vulgarity and meretriciousness that is so often associated with the familiar drawings in a similar field in Europe. The well-bred and healthy-minded American Girl is delightfully free from pose; mistress of herself she looks out upon the world with frankness and assurance . . . the Fisher young women are not showgirls, dress-maker's models or millinery exhibits, but the sort we associate with a May afternoon walk on upper Fifth Avenue or a day at the country club.'

With these new methods of print and illustration came new styles of fashion journalese. It was most noticeable in American magazines, such as *Vogue* and *Harper's Bazaar*, which used evocative 'word pictures' to convey the latest fashion news. Some of the more popular fashion magazines had not yet mastered or introduced the technique for coloured photographic reproduction – *Les Modes*'s use of colour photography was far too expensive, involving technology only available in specially equipped studios – but they regularly featured half-toned black and white photographs. In their way, these magazines had an impact on setting trends, since the camera lens didn't always compliment the free flowing Art Nouveau styles the couturiers wished to feature. Photography was not yet artistically up to the task of showing and selling fashion. It might have been the latest thing technologically, but from an aesthetic point of view, it was lacking. This prompted a desire for a new style of fashion magazine more suited to the new century, paradoxically using skills and techniques from earlier times and featuring quality fashion illustrations, to create something fresh with an entirely twentieth-century aesthetic.

The young Paris couturier Paul Poiret, who took a keen interest in the arts, was one of those who sought a new way to publicize his clothes. In 1908, he commissioned a little known artist, Paul Iribe, to illustrate a publicity album of designs, to be known as *Les Robes de Paul Poiret*. Iribe produced a masterly set of line drawings, which

ABOVE **Paul Iribe,** *Les Robes de Paul Poiret,* hand-coloured pochoir, 1908

were then highlighted with colour pigment applied by hand through fine, hand-cut stencils – a process called pochoir. It was developed for the Iribe album by the colourist Jean Saudé, who had learnt the basic technique while working as an apprentice on several albums of Art Nouveau textile designs with Eugène Grasset. Grasset also worked with quality chromolithography. *Les Mois*, in delicately coloured litho, is a good example of his fashionable illustrative style. Paul Iribe, born Paul Iribarnegaray in Angoulême, France in 1883, was one of the younger modernist illustrators who had studied at the École des Beaux Arts, starting his career with popular satirical magazines including *Le Rire*, *La Vie Parisienne* and *l'Assiette au Beurre*. Coco Chanel noted that 'no one could sketch an event more tellingly' than Paul Iribe. He was one of a talented group of like-minded illustrators who were beginning to come together at the time – young artists like George Barbier, Pierre Brissaud, Georges Martin and Jean Cocteau, who made the wry observation about Iribe's work for Paul Poiret that 'his album disgusts Mothers'. Such contentious opinions fueled public debate, providing the publicity that ultimately brought both Poiret and Iribe professional success and confirmed for the designer and his friend, the young publisher Lucien Vogel, the idea that successful and creative benefits were to be had by giving a freer rein to interesting, original artists.

BELOW Paul Iribe, *Les Modes*, photogravure, 1908

Vol. LXI   JUILLET, 1910   No. 1

LE MIROIR DES MODES

ÉDITÉ MENSUELLEMENT PAR

THE BUTTERICK PUBLISHING CO., PARIS, LONDRES, NEW-YORK

27, AVENUE DE L'OPÉRA, PARIS

PRIX DE L'ABONNEMENT: 10 FR. PAR AN.   POUR LES PAYS ÉTRANGERS: 12 FR.   PRIX DU NUMÉRO: 1 FR.

LEFT Frank Snapp, cover art for American magazine *Le Miroir des Modes*, photogravure, 1910

The 1900 Exposition, that glorious showcase for the Art Nouveau style, was also responsible for sowing the seeds of what would follow. One of the more popular pavilions had been that of the Russians. Thereafter, a series of concerts of Russian music, of gallery shows of Russian artists, books and articles, particularly in the fashion magazine *Femina*, paved the way for an interest in a culture that had an indigenous artistic tradition quite unlike anything in Western Europe. This Russian design influence began to have its effect on the new younger set of designers like Barbier, Martin, Iribe and Lucien Vogel, who via his involvement with the new and very fashion-conscious theatrical magazine, *Comœdia Illustré*, edited by Maurice de Brunhoff, designed most of the Russian influenced covers and promotional and publicity material. The new avant-garde designers had started to shake off all the constricting conventions of nineteenth-century design, and began experimenting with the simpler relationships to be found in geometric shapes, textural surfaces and angular forms that were, unexpectedly, to be found in the pochoir prints in Grasset's famous Art Nouveau folders, highlighted in contrasting colours. These unexpected 'finds' were combined with oriental ideals of quality and superb craftsmanship.

Between 1900 and 1910, a new style of fashionable design began to develop, which involved the intellectual as well as visual senses of both designers and their clients. The natural forms of Art Nouveau were maturing into a self-confident style to complement an era of scientific advance and rapidly developing technology. In America, the Wright brothers successfully flew the first engine-propelled aeroplane. In Germany, the Zeppelin completed trials and newly invented cars were being further developed. The young Albert Einstein was working on his theory of relativity; science and commerce were forging ahead. This allowed people the time and luxury of exploring their hidden depths, reading works by Sigmund Freud and Havelock Ellis's *Studies in the Psychology of Sex*, and questioning the social order, reading Vladimir Lenin's look at the social problems of the working class, *What Is To Be Done?*, and Thorstein Veblen's *Theory of the Leisure Classes*, all the while following the gossip, excesses and scandals of the great courts of Europe. But other events began to affect this comfortable, self-indulgent way of life – strikes, riots, attempted revolutions, assassinations and bomb attacks were besetting many major cities of Europe and, before long, would explode into the horrors of the First World War.

CHAPTER FIVE
THE ART DECO JAZZ AGE

I f, in 1910, you had found yourself, early on a Monday morning, near the Bourse du Commerce, you would have seen a crowd, many thousand strong, criss-crossing the Place de l'Opéra before disappearing down side streets into the small print ateliers and dingy workshops that generated the steady stream of illustrations for the world's fashion magazines and journals. These ateliers and workshops were situated in the midst of those run by the grand couturiers, whose army of seamstresses, beaders, cutters, fitters, embroiderers, tailors, milliners, button-makers and furriers contrived to fulfil the often elaborate decorative dreams and wishes of an ageing *haut monde.* Even during the fading belle époque, the essential energy of ideas needed by the designers and illustrators to create their fashion illustrations often came from unexpected or fortuitous sources.

Among older couture clients, yards and yards of luxurious fabrics, liberally trimmed with expensive lace and ribbons, were still the preference for evening dresses, in the manner of the hand-coloured fashion illustrations of their youth and in the Art Nouveau style that had been so all embracing at the time of the great Paris Exposition of 1900. But that design era was now rapidly evolving into something else, becoming something new. A group of young designers, artists and illustrators were working towards a more modernist style – a style that only became known as Art Deco in its later years, after the influential Paris Exhibition Internationale des Arts Décoratifs et Industriels Modernes, held in 1925.

The unique angular and boldly coloured early forms of Art Deco fashion were designed to compliment the natural shape and curves of the female body, which in 1910 was just beginning to escape the constrictions of the corset. This new, freer dress style was beautifully promoted by a number of illustrated deluxe albums, magazines,

LEFT Charles Martin, *Modes et Manières d'Aujourd'hui*, hand-coloured pochoir, 1913 portfolios, books and periodicals which both reflected and influenced the changes taking place in fashion and all other forms of design. The main attraction of these modernist Art Deco publications was their stylized fashion illustrations designed by young, avant-garde artists, many working under the guiding hand of the entrepreneur publishers, such as Lucien Vogel and, later, Jules Meynial. Their collective inventiveness and resplendent fashion images brilliantly captured the essence of the changing times. They were not, however, straightforward, line-for-line representations of designs produced by the great couture houses, as had often been the case in earlier fashion illustrations. Instead, each illustration was conceived by an individual artist as his own idiosyncratic interpretation of a couturier's design – an attempt to capture the spirit of the design rather that its surface detailing.

Lucien Vogel, the driving force behind many of these new deluxe publications, was born in Paris in 1886, the eldest child of a successful painter and illustrator. Raised among artists, he spent much of his childhood visiting the Paris art galleries and museums. By 1906, after studies in design and architecture, he began his professional career as an art director of the fashion magazine *Femina*. It was while working at *Femina* that he met the young couturier Paul Poiret. He was responsible for featuring several of Poiret's designs in the magazine and for introducing him to the illustrator Paul Iribe. In 1909, he worked for a time on the fashionable theatre magazine *Comædia Illustré*, most importantly on the promotional material for the first season of Diaghilev's Ballets Russes. Later, he was appointed editor of the influential *Art et Decoration* and married Cosette de Brunhoff, the daughter of his managing editor at *Comædia Illustré*. In 1910, Vogel undertook promotional design work for the second season of the Ballets Russes, staged at the grand opera house, for which he designed the opening night programme using a montage of illustrations by Léon Bakst. The events that followed were to have a huge impact on the emerging artists and fashion illustrators.

As Sergei Leonidovich Grigoriev, regisseur of Diaghilev's company, recorded in his memoirs: 'We were not much worried about *Le Carnaval*, the *Polovtsian Dances* and *Le Festin* . . . but *Scheherazade* in particular was new and complicated. It still needed finishing touches, there was all too little time and the dress rehearsal failed to go smoothly . . . Diaghilev remained relatively calm, believing in the maxim that a poor dress rehearsal augurs a good first night.' Diaghilev was proved right. *Scheherazade* was much more than a success – it was a sublime triumph. The largely untrained but beautifully sensual Ida Rubinstein in the leading role created a sensation, with one critic writing, 'She

RIGHT Léon Bakst, Ballets Russes costume design, *Comædia Illustré*, photogravure, 1912

4ᵉ Année
Nᵒ 15
1ᵉʳ Mai 1912

PRIX :
1 franc
48 Pages

COMOEDIA

ILLUSTRÉ

"Hélène de Sparte"
au
Châtelet

Mme IDA RUBINSTEIN
dans le rôle d'Hélène

Aquarelle de
Léon BAKST

Aquarelle originale de BAKST

LEFT & ABOVE *La Femme Chic*, hand-coloured
lithograph, 1912

LEFT Simon Puget, *La Gazette du Bon Ton*, hand-coloured pochoir, 1914

ABOVE LEFT Victor Lhuer, *Le Journal des Dames et des Modes*, hand-coloured pochoir, 1914

ABOVE RIGHT George Barbier, *La Gazette du Bon Ton*, hand-coloured pochoir, 1912

blend of art, fashion and sex that swept all before it. The Paris public, it seemed, could not get enough.

Léon Bakst was born Lev Samoilovich Rosenberg in 1866 and studied in St Petersburg before going to Paris in 1890 to complete his training. It was in Paris where he adopted his grandmother's maiden name, Bakst. On his return to St Petersburg, he was appointed an official painter to the imperial family and was introduced to Sergei Diaghilev by Prince Volkonsky, the director of the Imperial Theatre. The prince wanted them to work together on Diaghilev's journal, *World of Art*, and they quickly formed a creative partnership, pulling in other talented young painters and designers to work on productions at the Bolshoi Theatre in Moscow, before setting their sights on Paris.

A number of Bakst costume illustrations were featured on the cover of *Comœdia Illustré* over the two heady years following the Ballets Russes' triumphant first season. Many more appeared as double-page spreads. At the same time, *Comœdia Illustré*, sensing

ABOVE & RIGHT   Pierre Brissaud, *La Gazette du Bon Ton*,
hand-coloured pochoir, 1914

ABOVE George Barbier, *La Gazette du Bon Ton*, hand-coloured pochoir, 1914

ABOVE H. Robert Dammy, *La Gazette du Bon Ton*, hand-coloured pochoir, 1913

ABOVE   Maria Likarz, *Wiener Werkstätte*, linocut, 1914

ABOVE Irene 'Reni' Schaschl, *Wiener Werkstätte*, linocut, 1914

the shift in the public mood, featured articles on Loïe Fuller, Isadora Duncan and the more progressive couturiers and milliners. The magazine covers featured designs by Jeanne Paquin and a young Gabrielle (not yet 'Coco') Chanel. Others were designed by the likes of Paul Iribe, whose cover harked back to his album, *Les Robes de Paul Poiret*. Poiret's wife and muse, Denise, had discarded the corset (as had her friend Cosette Vogel) and for her, the personification of the new and liberated woman, *la garçonne*, Poiret designed wonderfully exotic clothes that allowed for natural body shapes and freedom of movement. This abandonment of the corset was, in the eyes and minds of respectable society, tantamount to being naked – which was exactly why it became desirable. No young or fashionable woman wanted to look like a relic from the 1890s belle époque, and so Poiret's success was assured.

This new desire of women to assume the sensuality of their natural shape, mixed with the eroticsm of Bakst and *Scheherezade*, would, according to critics, breach the bounds of respectability. The depth of social repression at the time, left over from the previous century, made this all the more electrifying. Critics and traditionalists were appalled to see even 'respectable' women painting their faces and throwing

BELOW Pierre Brissaud, *La Gazette du Bon Ton*, hand-coloured pochoir, 1914
RIGHT Etienne Drian, *La Gazette du Bon Ton*, San Francisco exhibition special edition, hand-coloured pochoir, 1915–16
FAR RIGHT Gerda Wegener, *Le Journal des Dames et des Modes*, hand-coloured pochoir, 1914

off their corsets and layers of undergarments, so that they too could wear the new, figure revealing dresses. Even more horrifying, these women were demanding the right to vote, to smoke in public, to dance the forbidden tango, to wear sports clothes that showed their legs, even one-piece bathing costumes. Other aspects of western life had also been changing. The film industry in North America and Europe by 1912 had regular weekly audiences of many millions and new films seemed to have the power to change people's ideas and ideals overnight. The sewing machine and methods of mass production had made modern clothing available to an ever-increasing population. Cars were becoming larger, faster and more numerous. Airplanes could now fly great distances, linking major cities in a matter of hours. Trains were transporting more and more passengers across the vastness of Europe, Russia, India and parts of Africa, Canada and the United States. Ships were larger and more comfortable, enabling more people to travel abroad. And each year, more than a million people from the poorer, working classes were leaving Europe and parts of Great Britain in the hope of finding a better life in the United States, Canada, South Africa and Australia.

For a young art director and publisher, this was exactly the moment for which he had been waiting. Lucien Vogel, so the story goes, conceived the idea for his new publication, *La Gazette du Bon Ton*, while staying with his wife at the home of her cousin. Early one morning and noticing the paintings on the bedroom wall lit by the rising sun, he asked his wife, Cosette, if she had ever seen more beautiful fashion drawings. They decided, then and there, to produce

ABOVE   George Barbier, *La Gazette du Bon Ton*, San Francisco exhibition
special edition, hand-coloured pochoir, 1915–16

G. BARBIER 1914

George Barbier, *Modes et Manières d'Aujourd'hui*, hand-coloured pochoir, 1914; George Barbier, *Le Journal des Dames et des Modes*, hand-coloured pochoir, 1914; George Barbier, *Le Bonheur du Jour*, hand-coloured pochoir, 1924

a magazine that would showcase such creative talent. Those paintings were by Pierre Brissaud and Bernard Boutet de Monvel, and around them the Vogels began to gather a stable of other young artists, many from the same École des Beaux Arts. The chosen group would soon include George Barbier, André Marty, Charles Martin, Georges Lepape and Francisco Javier Gosé.

At this time, Paul Poiret moved to avenue d'Antin and started the Martine design atelier. He was a master showman with a perfect sense of timing and to launch his establishment he gave a costume party, designed as a spectacular Persian extravaganza, inviting 300 guests to come to his 'The Thousand and Second Night' dressed as ancient Persians, reserving, of course, the role of Sultan for himself. Dressed in a fur-trimmed caftan and wearing a jewelled turban, Poiret presided over his fairytale fête from an elaborate throne. Behind, in a gilded cage, his 'beautiful favourites', playing the part of harem girls, watched the guests arrive and take in the magnificent set Poiret had created in the courtyard and grounds of his eighteenth-century mansion. The gardens were filled with ibis, peacocks and flamingos freely wandering among the lantern-hung trees, in which parrots, macaws and monkeys were tethered. An old Persian marketplace – filled with slave-traders, cobblers, tailors, sweetmeat sellers, fortune-tellers, even beggars – was recreated, the backdrops and awnings painted by artists including Raoul Dufy. Middle Eastern cooks prepared exotic dishes and handsome 'slaves' served drinks to delighted guests as they watched, from silken cushions, dancing girls and musicians. The high point of the evening came when the Sultan threw open his 'cage of favourites' and out stepped Madame Poiret wearing her husband's latest creation. She was dressed in loosely cut harem pants of white and ochre chiffon, fitted tightly at the waist and ankles, under a short hooped tunic of gauzy gold lamé, topped by a lamé turban, fastened with a turquoise clasp and a tall feather, which gave her the look of an exotic flower.

The effect of this spectacular was enormous and Poiret's Oriental Collection was an instant success. Within days, it was reported that his salon was filled with the fashionable ladies of Paris ordering copies of his lampshade tunic and his harem pantaloons. Although some critics described his new style as 'vulgar, wicked and ugly' his designs finally freed women from that last shackle of the previous age – the hobble (or, as it has been called, the 'hobble, toddle, toil and wobble') skirt. In hindsight, it was clear that Parisians had been flirting with oriental influences and the exotic long before the beginning of the century, but it took the impact of the Ballets Russes and the flair of Paul Poiret and others to weave it all together and lift it to heights of magnificent beauty.

ABOVE & RIGHT Charles Martin, *La Gazette du Bon Ton*,
hand-coloured pochoir, 1913

During the following months, Lucien and Cosette Vogel devoted themselves to searching out talent for their new venture. Edna Woolman Chase, then editor of *Vogue*, said of this young band of artists in her 1954 autobiography, *Always in Vogue*: 'Talent they had in plenty; their business instincts were nil. Their good fortune was to meet with Lucien Vogel, publisher, press agent, wet nurse and catalyst, who formed them into a cohesive unit and created for them a shop window in his proposed *La Gazette du Bon Ton* . . . Vogel's idea of displaying their art and splitting the magazine's profits had appealed to the gifted spirits until he one day advanced a little proposition which evoked a furore.' He proposed that the new magazine would be sponsored by the seven leading couturiers – Chéruit, Doeuillet, Doucet, Lanvin, Poiret, Redfern and Worth – and that each artist would draw one of each backer's designs for publication in the magazine. According to Woolman Chase, 'this first sniff of trade outraged the geniuses, yet it was a sound idea, for it would flatter the sponsors and give a certain journalistic and serviceable quality to a project that, if it remained in the realm of pure art might wither before its flowering.' She continued that, although his group of artists 'cried out that they were creators and originators, Papa Lucien talked to them like a French uncle, enunciating little phrases about francs and sous and in no time all the boys came round.'

In fact, they reached a compromise. It was agreed that each artist could design and publish one picture of his own choosing for every illustration of a fashion designed by one of the couturiers. Under Vogel's direction, the artists set to work to develop a new and distinctive style of fashion illustration – the 'story-telling pictures' for which the *Gazette* was to become famous. The magazine was designed to appeal to the *haut monde* and the art connoisseurs of the period, to be 'a truly modern review of art and fashion, and an exact record of the fashionable life of our time'. A typeface was designed to complement the pochoir plates and layout. Special paper was selected and leading writers and poets were engaged as contributors. On 15 November 1912, *La Gazette du Bon Ton* was published to instant acclaim. Inside, Lucien Vogel laid out his manifesto – his aims and hopes for his new magazine: 'We have called this magazine *La Gazette du Bon Ton*. To be '*de Bon Ton*', elegance is not enough. There are a hundred ways of being elegant; good taste is the same for all. Elegance changes – '*le Bon Ton*' does not, it follows fashion and taste. '*Le Bon Ton*' is not formal, yet it is reserved. It is not dull, yet it is discreet. Its hallmark is an innate sense of grace – guided by this, all things are permitted . . . *La Gazette du Bon Ton* intends to revive the charming tradition of fashion journals of the past. We have some worthy predecessors.' Here Vogel listed *La Galerie*

ABOVE Costume illustration by George Barbier, hand-coloured pochoir, 1918

PAULETTE DUVAL

GEORGE BARBIER 1920

ABOVE **Costume illustration by George Barbier, hand-coloured pochoir, 1920**

des Modes, followed by *Cabinet des Modes*, which he considered the very first fashion magazines. He mentioned the copycats and spin-offs across Europe, continuing on to the publication of La Mésangère's *Journal des Dames*, saying, 'These collections, charming though they may be, would seem very old fashioned today. A new age and new methods demand new publications. And yet, the entire public today, like that of the eighteenth century, is interested in fashion.'

Having gathered together his stable of artists – Bakst, Barbier, Bernard and Maurice Boutet de Monvel, Brissaud, Brunelleschi, Carlège, Caro-Delvaille, Dresa, Abel Faivre, Gosé, Iribe, Lepape, Maggie, Charles Martin and André Marty – he found a printing method worthy of such an ambitious project. The use of colour stencilling was not new in Paris, with its long established studios churning out hand-coloured fashion plates, often with quality suffering as a result of quantity. But although the colouring of such plates was often crude and the registration of the final stencilling generally poor because of the speed required to maintain the flow of production, the method did provide a training ground for many of the later pochoir artisans. Undoubtedly the exhibitions of Japanese stencil-printed textiles, held in Paris during the 1880s and 1890s, had helped to renew interest in the art of pochoir printing. Some of the young French printmakers looked to the Japanese art of fabric stencilling as they sought to revitalize the art of book illustration, which at the time was suffering from monochromatic uniformity – the result of a focus on photomechanical

ABOVE LEFT TO RIGHT Etienne Drian, *Le Journal des Dames et des Modes*, hand-coloured pochoir, 1913; George Barbier, *La Gazette du Bon Ton*, hand-coloured pochoir, 1913; Umberto Brunelleschi, *Le Journal des Dames et des Modes*, hand-coloured pochoir, 1914
RIGHT George Barbier, *Le Journal des Dames et des Modes*, hand-coloured pochoir, 1914

ABOVE Loeze, *Le Journal des Dames et des Modes*, hand-coloured pochoir, 1913

ABOVE RIGHT V. Jonois, *Le Journal des Dames et des Modes*, hand-coloured pochoir, 1913

RIGHT Armand Vallée, *Le Journal des Dames et des Modes*, hand-coloured pochoir, 1913

OVERLEAF Illustration for fur catalogue by Victor Lhuer, lithograph coloured engraving, 1915

ABOVE   George Barbier, *La Gazette du Bon Ton*, hand-coloured pochoir, 1922

ABOVE George Barbier, *La Gazette du Bon Ton*, hand-coloured pochoir, 1921

LEFT George Barbier, *La Gazette du Bon Ton*, hand-coloured pochoir, 1921

ABOVE George Barbier, *Le Bonheur du Jour*, hand-coloured pochoir, 1920

printing techniques. Pochoir, with its adroit use of pigments applied by hand through finely cut stencils, was an artistic revelation.

One such printmaker was Jean Saudé, who, in the early 1890s, worked with Eugène Grasset and Maurice Pillard Verneuil on the some of the first Art Nouveau design portfolios. He was greatly impressed by the kimono fabrics and ukiyo-e prints at the Paris Exhibition of 1880 and was lucky to be able to inspect some and to question the Japanese artisans, from whom he discovered the intricacies of Japanese stencil making. From these observations and the experience gained by working with Grasset, Saudé began developing his own technique, which he later detailed in his *Traité d'Eluminure d'Art au Pochoir*, published in 1925. In their foreward and introduction to this book, Antoine Bourdelle and Georges Goursat wrote that they had witnessed how, with dedication and skill, Saudé could recreate even the most complex illustrations: 'The nuances, the delicate shades, the washes and the running of the watercolours, the white reserves, even the repainting and corrections, down to the very subtlest values, the entire image is carried out with a perfection that creates a total illusion of the original. One can even feel the brushstrokes.' Édouard Bénédictus added in a note to the foreword that it was to 'the ingenuity and talent of M. Saudé that we owe our knowledge of certain kinds of new art,

ABOVE & RIGHT George Barbier, *Falbalas et Fanfreluches*,
hand-coloured pochoir, 1923

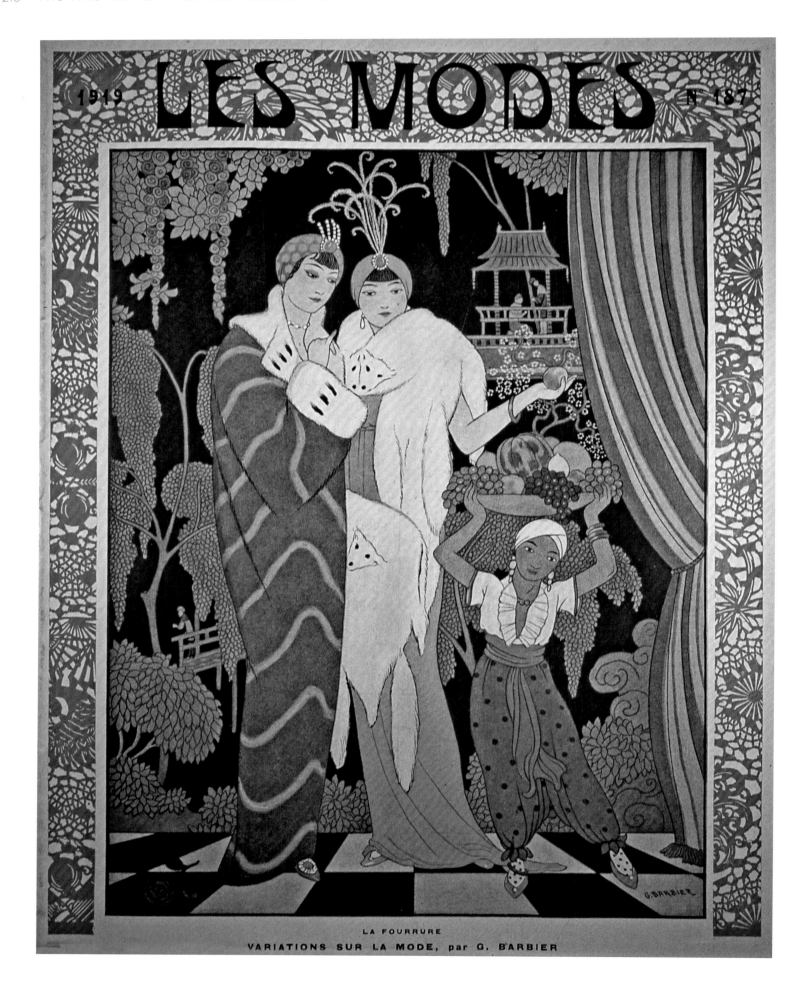

LA FOURRURE
VARIATIONS SUR LA MODE, par G. BARBIER

LEFT   George Barbier, cover art for *Les Modes*, photogravure, 1919

RIGHT   Léon Bonnotte, *La Guirlande: Album d'Art et de Littérature*, hand-coloured pochoir, *c.*1920

which without his pochoir process might have remained unknown to us because they were unreproduceable by any other process'.

Saudé's process involved three major steps, each demanding a good eye and meticulous craftsmanship. First, the original illustration was analysed and broken down into its constituent parts and translated into a wood engraving, an etching or a lithoprint. Then, each colour area was analysed so that accurately cut stencils could be made. In the final step, the original colours were matched to the printer's selection of opaque, translucent or transparent colours and then a base substance used to achieve the correct viscosity. The order of printing and the method of applying the chosen colours were then

determined. Trial prints were made in order to test the accuracy of the stencils over the background drawing and at this stage the artist would approve the pochoir print, their signature being added only after all the adjustments had been made.

Generally between 150 to 350 pochoir copies were printed for a deluxe portfolio, with up to 2,000 being printed for magazines like *La Gazette du Bon Ton* or *Le Journal des Dames et des Modes*. Each print of each separate issue could involve up to thirty-two stencils. Thus, a deluxe collection of twenty such prints involved nearly 450 separate stencils, in order to accurately reproduce exact facsimiles of the artist's original work. This then had to be repeated 250 or more times to achieve the total print run – a very labour intensive method of printing. Saudé was not the only pochoirist working in Paris in the early 1900s. Greningaire et Fils, where Saudé apprenticed, was still active, their name appearing on many fine books and albums of the day. Others include Ranson et Fils, E. Charpentier, Gustave Raynal, Tolmer et Cie and Vangirard et Cie, who printed the pochoir for the *Gazette's* rival, *Le Journal des Dames et des Modes* – the first regularly published deluxe limited-edition fashion magazine to contain quality pochoir prints of the 'latest fashions as conceived by the grand couturiers and drawn by the leading artists of the period'. It was available by subscription only, direct from the publishers, and between June 1912 and August 1914, seventy-nine editions were published. The print run was limited to 1,250 numbered copies – the first twelve were printed on cream Japon paper, delicate and difficult to handle, with a faint shell-like pearly sheen that did not allow the gouache colour to soak

ABOVE LEFT Eduardo García Benito, *La Gazette du Bon Ton*, hand-coloured pochoir, *c.*1920

ABOVE MIDDLE, ABOVE & RIGHT Fernand Siméon, *La Gazette du Bon Ton*, hand-coloured pochoir, 1920

ABOVE Arrangement by Jean Saudé, *La Gazette du Bon Ton*, hand-coloured pochoir, *c*.1920

in, allowing it to lie on the surface and 'sparkle with the freshness of petals'. The rest were printed on the best quality handmade paper. Copies were mailed to subscribers in London, New York, Rome, St Petersburg, Rio, Buenos Aires and Berlin. Like the *Gazette*, *Le Journal des Dames et des Modes* was conceived as a twentieth-century version of the famous eighteenth-century publication of the same name, which first appeared in 1797, as fashionable Paris was beginning to recover after the bloody Revolution. In the new version, publisher Jacques de Nouvion paid tribute to his predecessor, La Mésangère, including a facsimile plate from 1812 in his first issue, along with two contemporary fashion plates and eight pages of text.

Le Journal des Dames et des Modes and the first edition of Vogel's *Gazette du Bon Ton* were quickly followed by the first annual edition of the luxurious album *Modes et Manières d'Aujourd'hui*, containing twelve sumptuous illustrations by Georges Lepape. Published by Pierre Corrard and printed by Marquet et Cie, the pochoir was again done by Jean Saudé, who had also been responsible for the 1911 album for the House of Paquin, *L'Eventail de la Fourrure*, which featured drawings by Iribe and George Barbier. Like the *Journal des Dames* and the *Gazette*, these special albums were intended as showcases for the new fashions. They combined the luxury of beautiful materials

ABOVE Eduardo García Benito,
L'Homme Elegant, hand-coloured
pochoir, 1920

and superb craftsmanship with an artistic excellence that even the most fastidious connoisseur could not fail to appreciate. It was obvious that these publications and those that were to follow in the next few years – *Luxe de Paris, Le Goût du Jour, La Guirlande: Album d'Art et de Littérature, Les Feuillets d'Art, La Guirlande des Mois, Falbalas et Fanfreluches, Les Douze Mois de l'Année* and many others – were not just fashion magazines, as we understand the term today; they were what an editorial in *The Studio* magazine described as 'a monument to the taste of the age'.

The British publisher William Heinemann, who purchased the rights for an English edition of the *Gazette*, introduced this French deluxe publication to English readers by announcing in an introductory leaflet: 'Here is no confusion of tints inevitable in photographic reproduction; but each picture is hand-coloured exactly in imitation of the artist's original – a real picture, in fact, not a mere reflection of lifeless mannequins . . . *La Gazette du Bon Ton* is an expensive publication, expensive to produce and expensive in its aim to be the true mirror of all that is smartest and most elegant in the social life of our day.'

In the years between 1912 and 1914, it became widely acknowledged that although the couturiers of the rue de la Paix were creators of the individual fashion styles, it was the fashion illustrators who were the true inventors. It was they who brought to life new images that permeated the imagination of their readers and subscribers and made them long for more new ideas. As an editorial in *La Gazette du Bon Ton* stated at the time: 'Artists today are in part the inventors of fashion; what doesn't fashion owe to Iribe, who introduced to it simplicity of line and an oriental flavour, or to Drian, or to Bakst?'

The idea behind these and the other pochoir publications was, in Vogel's words, to 'revive the tradition of fashionable journalism of the eighteenth century, in order to forget the events and absurdities of the nineteenth'. Numerous editorials made reference to the fashion illustrations of Watteau, Leclerc, Saint-Aubin, Desrais and Vernet and the work of publisher Pierre de La Mésangère, but, well aware that they were living in the twentieth century and not the eighteenth, they did not attempt to simply copy the style of those earlier publications. Instead, they declared that 'a new age and new methods of production, demand new publications.'

In addition to the pochoir fashion illustrations, such publications contained articles by many of the most popular, prolific and witty authors of the day, among them Jean Cocteau, André de Fouquières, Marcel Boulanger, René Blum, the novelists Anatole France, Marcel Proust and Paul Margueritte, the poet Fernand Gregh, the dramatists Pierre Veber and Henri Lavedan and the composer Erik Satie, who wrote on a wide variety of subjects. Their fascinating range of narrative styles was a fitting complement for the range of illustrative styles.

The illustrators, like the writers, were a varied group of people who came from all over Europe to live and work in Paris. Umberto Brunelleschi, for instance, moved from Tuscany to Paris in 1900, where he became well known as a printer, book illustrator and costume designer. Between 1912 and 1914 and later, from 1919 to 1921, he regularly contributed to several of the prestigious fashion publications, before becoming a set and costume designer in France, Italy and America. Spanish-born Francisco Javier Gosé, after studying in Barcelona, arrived in Paris and established a small studio in 1901. His early illustrations appeared regularly in such magazines as *Le Rire*, *L'Assiette au Beurre* and *Simplicissimus* before he began working for both the *Journal des Dames* and the *Gazette*.

The French illustrator Pierre Brissaud was born in Paris in 1885. He studied painting, illustration and engraving at the École des Beaux Arts and from 1910 supplied an increasing number of illustrations for deluxe books, popular magazines and exclusive fashion publications. His close associate and cousin, Bernard Boutet de Monvel, was also born in Paris in 1885. His studies completed, he began illustrating for *Le Rire*, *L'Assiette au Beurre* and *La Vie Parisienne*. Later, at the

ABOVE *La Gazette du Bon Ton*, Golden Edition,

hand-coloured pochoir, 1925

ABOVE & RIGHT **Anni Offterdinger**, *Styl*, hand-coloured pochoir, 1923; 1922

suggestion of Paul Poiret, for whom he designed a range of menswear, he became one of the early contributors to *La Gazette du Bon Ton* and subsequently to *Vogue* and *Harper's Bazaar*.

Georges Lepape also studied at the École des Beaux Arts, forming a strong bond with others there at the same time, such as André Marty, Charles Martin and Bernard Boutet de Monvel. In 1910 he was commissioned by Paul Poiret to create another album, *Les Choses de Paul Poiret*, assuring his future and reputation as one of the leading fashion illustrators of his day.

Arguably the greatest illustrator of this period, and certainly one of the most prolific, was George Barbier, whose work appeared regularly in many of the leading pochoir publications. Born in Nantes, he completed his art studies at the Paris École des Beaux Arts, joining friends like Iribe and Lepape and his two cousins, Pierre Brissaud

FAR LEFT & RIGHT Robert Leonard, *Styl*,
hand-coloured pochoir, 1922
LEFT Anni Offterdinger, *Styl*, hand-
coloured pochoir, 1923

and Bernard Boutet de Monvel, forming what *Vogue* later called 'The
Knights of the Bracelet'. He developed a love of Greek antiquity, which
he later combined with erotic and sensual sophistication, a strong
and sure line and a love of oriental colour and detail. His sense of
luxury, tinged with erotic decadence and wry humour, became the
hallmarks of his work and it proved to be a popular cocktail, winning
him commissions in a huge number of publications – magazines,
portfolios and the deluxe books he created with master engraver and
printer François-Louis Schmied.

The principal backers of the new Art Deco style were often involved
in some aspect of the style themselves – the couturiers Jacques Doucet,
Madeleine Vionnet, Jeanne Lanvin and Paul Poiret were buying Art
Deco objects as well as designing the new and revolutionary Art Deco
fashions. Knowledgeable patrons expressed their admiration for the
new group of designers and fashion illustrators, whom they perceived
to be pursuing their aesthetic dreams with a single-mindedness
worthy of the master craftsmen of the past, encouraging the belief
that western design was entering a twentieth-century Renaissance.
'Not since that Golden Age of 500 years earlier,' it was proclaimed,
'had so many artists, designers and master craftsmen devoted so
much creative energy to such an abundance of beautiful artifacts.'
The Commissaire-Générale de l'Exposition Internationale who had
been responsible for the Paris Exposition of 1900 proposed that an
Exposition Internationale des Arts Décoratifs be held in Paris in 1914
to celebrate this culmination of the modern movement. Unfortunately,

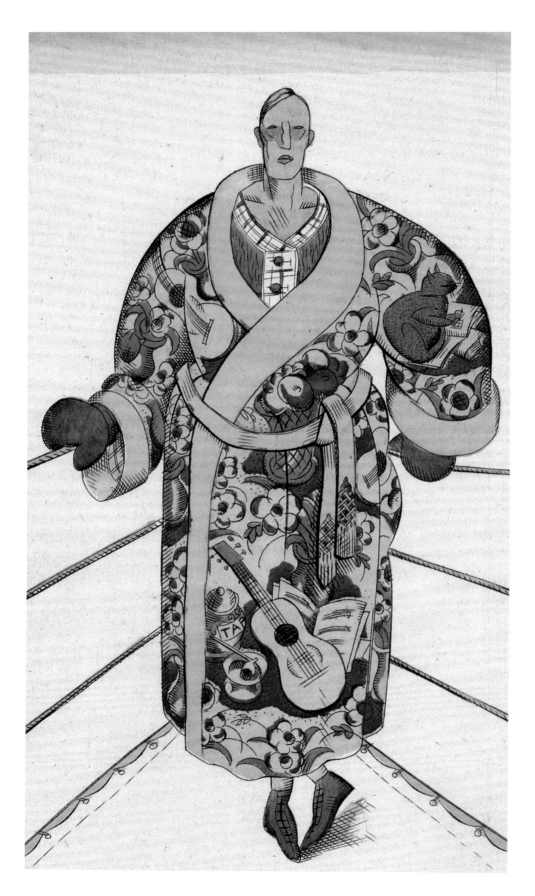

ABOVE Eduardo García Benito, *Le Goût du Jour*, hand-coloured pochoir, 1920

RIGHT Fernand Siméon, *Modes et Manières d'Aujourd'hui*, hand-coloured pochoir, 1922

the outbreak of the First World War in 1914 forced the postponement of the exhibition until 1925, when it would be enlarged to include industrially made products, a decision that would ultimately be its downfall.

But, between 1910 and the outbreak of war at the beginning of August 1914, the new *style moderne* was gathering pace and followers. Skilled artists and craftsmen from all over the world came to Paris, bringing with them their talent and their own cultural influences to add to the mix. The origins of Art Deco grew out of the ideas of nineteenth-century designers such as Christopher Dresser and Michael Thonet, from the theories of William Morris, Walter Crane and members of the British Arts and Craft movement, the Secessionists, Jugendstil, the Wiener Werkstätte and the aestheticism of Japanese master craftsmen. With contributions from artists, architects and designers across Europe – like Henry van de Velde, Josef Hoffmann, Koloman Moser, Peter Behrens and Charles Rennie Mackintosh – with the colours of the Fauves and the visual strength of Léon Bakst and Diaghilev's Ballets Russes, the writings of Sigmund Freud and Havelock Ellis, Western Europe had shifted, throwing off the overbearing and outdated mores, morals and merchandise of the previous century.

ABOVE LEFT   Fernand Siméon, *La Gazette du Bon Ton*, hand-coloured pochoir, 1921

ABOVE   Illustration from French sales brochure, photogravure, 1920s

The great fashion designers of the new mode – Paul Poiret, Gabrielle 'Coco' Chanel, Paul Iribe, Madeleine Vionnet – together with Jean Dunand, Jacques-Emile Ruhlmann, René Lalique, François-Louis Schmied, Pierre Legrain, Eileen Gray and others, decided that to achieve a consistent aesthetic standard in their products, only natural materials of the finest quality should be used. The designs were to be original in concept and made with the skill of the finest craftsmen available. The end product was exclusive, luxurious and expensive and sold to wealthy collectors from all over the world.

An embryonic version of this new Art Deco style first appeared in the summer of 1915, when, in the midst of war, the Paris couturiers who had not been called up to fight or for essential work decided to hold an exhibition of their latest wartime fashions at the 1915 San Francisco Panama-Pacific International Exposition, to help boost French finances by increasing overseas demand for their fashionable merchandise. To promote the exhibition, the publishers of *La Gazette du Bon Ton*, who had closed down their activities with the outbreak of war, produced a special deluxe edition containing twelve sumptuous illustrations by Drian, Lepape and Barbier, who were released from wartime service to undertake the task. One month after its publication in June 1915, a facsimile edition was published by Condé Nast, the publisher of *Vogue*, using mechanically coloured fashion plates instead of pochoir and including the only photographs ever used in any of these luxury publications.

In this wartime edition of *La Gazette du Bon Ton*, the editors proudly stated: 'Although a part of French soil is yet in the hands of the invaders, Paris remains as ever the Paris of good taste and fashion. Therefore, in spite of the glorious trials of war, and in order that Paris may retain her accustomed rank in every Exposition, the following great and justly renowned dress-makers have sent to San Francisco their latest and most stylish creations – Beer, Callot Soeurs, Chéruit, Doeuillet, Doucet, Jenny, Jeanne Lanvin, Martial et Armand, Paquin, Premet, Worth.' In August 1915, Lucien Vogel launched a new deluxe magazine, *Le Style Parisien*, aimed at the American market and intended to further boost French fashion exports. But for the duration of the war, regular production of the deluxe publications had to be suspended.

The Armistice was signed in 1918. Devastated European nations, finally at peace, began to pick up the pieces. The fashionable life of the wealthy began to regain its momentum, but even to the rich, who could travel the world enjoying luxury and leisure, life no longer seemed to follow the traditions of unquestioned authority and privilege. The war changed many aspects of life at all levels of society. The change

Deuxième Année. — Nº 19.   REVUE BIMENSUELLE   Jeudi 30 Juin 1921.

L'ILLUSTRATION
DES MODES
Lucien Vogel Directeur

Une Robe pour les Courses, de DŒUILLET.

Prix du Numéro : 2 fr. 30.   15, Rue Saint-Georges, Paris.

LEFT & ABOVE Mario Simon, cover art for *L'Illustration des Modes*, photogravure, 1921

was most obvious for the younger generation, as they had been most affected by the horrors of the war. Young women, no longer needed to man posts in factories, hospitals and offices, were free to bob their hair, paint their faces and emulate movie stars like Theda Bara or Mae Murray, those women who had made such an impression during the drab, fraught years of the war. The young men, on the other hand, those survivors of the bloody conflict, sought release in almost frenetic amusement and gaiety. Together, these young men and women began to dance to the rhythm of jazz.

At war's end, many of the African-American ex-servicemen found their way to Paris, a city comparatively free of racial prejudice. By the early 1920s they were joined by an increasing number of well-known jazz musicians, flocking to Paris to play in night clubs and music halls. White musicians and composers began to incorporate these jazz rhythms into their music as it seemed to best capture the mood of the moment. The sense of relief that the grim struggle was over mingled with the bewildered realization that there would be no returning to the tranquil, golden days of the belle époque. Many Europeans were exhausted, both physically and mentally, by the war. Many were near or past bankruptcy, while some had profited hugely as a result of the conflict. If ever there was a time that demanded change, this post-war period was it – so, to the new beat set by the jazz musicians, designers and illustrators sketched out a new future for the survivors of the world's first global conflict.

By this time, almost 10,000 Americans had joined the ranks of millionaires and a surprising number of the French, German and British had profited too, joining what remained of the pre-war *beau monde*. This combination of nobility, old money and nouveau riche, enlivened by the addition of international authors, playwrights, artists and composers, rapidly became acceptable in the new world of wealth and high fashion. All of this provided London and Paris with much needed vitality and supplied the couturiers and craftsmen with a new clientele. In 1919, to cater to this lucrative market, two new fashion magazines appeared, both beautifully illustrated in high quality pochoir in the Art Deco style – *La Guirlande: Album d'Art et de Littérature*, limited to 800 copies per month, under the guiding hand of Umberto Brunelleschi, and *Les Feuillets d'Art*, Lucien Vogel's new venture. *La Gazette du Bon Ton* reappeared as a regular monthly magazine in February 1920.

At the beginning of the 1920s, the traffic of ideas between the United States and Europe was opening up as never before. A steady stream of new music, film and entertainment flowed eastward from America to enliven war-weary Europe. Art Deco artifacts and *objets d'art* were shipped westward, to add a touch of European culture to

the New World. Everywhere, society strove to be brilliant and youthful, although the brazen manners and habits of the 'bright young things', as the younger generation came to be called, shocked and outraged their elders, who filled newspapers and other publications with letters of complaint. Nevertheless, the young at the beginning of the new decade were rightfully, even pointedly, beginning to exercise their freedom. In Britain after the war, women, at least those over thirty, could vote; the first woman, American-born Lady Astor, was elected to the House of Commons; several of the famous universities opened their doors to women students and family planning clinics brought hopes of sexual freedom and condemnation in equal measure.

William Heinemann again began to market *La Gazette du Bon Ton*. His sales brochure proclaimed that his fashion magazine, *The Queen*, would 'publish the first number of the new series of this, the most beautiful magazine in the world. Publication was suspended during the war, for most of its contributors were called to the colours. Those of them who survive, including the Directing Editor, M. Lucien Vogel,

ABOVE   Guy Arnoux, *Les Femmes de ce Temps*, pochoir over woodcut, 1920

RIGHT   Guy Arnoux, cover art for *Monsieur*, hand-coloured pochoir, 1922

LEFT Marthe Romme, *La Guirlande: Album d'Art et de Littérature*, hand-coloured pochoir, 1919

ABOVE Marthe Romme, *Calendrier Républicain*, hand-coloured pochoir, 1919

will be associated in the production of the new series with other brilliant artists and chroniqueurs . . . it is as sumptuous as art and craftsmanship can make it. Its ambition is to be a mirror and a record of whatever is most elegant in the social life of our day. As a review of fashion, *La Gazette du Bon Ton* was the first publication to bring the pictorial artist into collaboration with the dress designer . . . delicately coloured by hand, each of the new plates will portray a dress chosen from the newest models of the great maisons de couture, presenting at the same time a charming picture of contemporary life in its own appropriate setting . . . They show modern life – especially life in Paris – as set forth by those who all others are best able to appreciate and to interpret its charm.'

Another deluxe fashion magazine appeared at the beginning of 1920. *Le Goût du Jour* was limited to 1,400 numbered copies, and introduced a new group of fashion illustrators who also worked for the *Gazette*, among them Raoul Dufy, Edouard Halouze, Marthe Romme, Eduardo García Benito, Fernand Siméon, Mario Simon, José Zinoview, Marcelle Pichon, Robert Bonfils, Thayaht and Janine Aghion. Some of the well known pre-war artists continued as contributors: illustrations by George Barbier, André Marty and Charles Martin were regularly featured. The changing mood was reflected in new emphasis being given in the text to contemporary lifestyles, travel, the theatre and music, with articles on 'Le jazz

ABOVE Charles Martin, *La Gazette du Bon Ton*,
hand-coloured pochoir, 1920

ABOVE **Robert Bonfils**, *Modes et Manières d'Aujourd'hui*,
hand-coloured pochoir over woodcut, 1920

ABOVE & RIGHT **Paul Allier,** *L'Hiver* from *Quatre Saisons*,
hand-coloured pochoir, mid-1920s

3e Année

NOËL

LEFT Cover art for *Art-Goût-Beauté*,
hand-coloured pochoir, 1923

RIGHT Georges Gillroy, cover art for *Le Jardin des Modes*, photogravure, 1925

Le Jardin des Modes

Lucien Vogel, Directeur

Americain' and 'Le mouvement moderne'. Lucien Vogel also started a glossy magazine, *L'Illustration des Modes*, featuring both fashion illustrations and photography, as a rival to both *Vogue* and *Harper's Bazaar*, both of which had wooed several of Vogel's original artists, using them to create particularly memorable covers – notably Georges Lepape for *Vogue* and Erté for *Harper's Bazaar*. Vogel also published a number of limited-edition deluxe books and folders, one of which, *Sports et Divertissements*, was illustrated in Cubist style by Charles Martin.

During the 1920s, the glossy magazines – *L'Officiel*, *La Femme Chic*, *Les Elégances Parisiennes*, *Vogue*, *Harper's Bazaar*, *Excelsior Modes* and *Femina* – began to develop their own unique styles, featuring many of the leading photographers of the period like Edward Steichen, Adolph de Meyer, Paul O'Doyé and Moisson together with

the work of the pochoir fashion illustrators. The influence of these publications was growing, and as their circulation increased so did the number of advertisers anxious to reach their growing and affluent readership. Lucien Vogel noted this change of fashion emphasis and decided to sell the *Gazette* to the American publisher Condé Nast, to help finance his new project, *L'Illustration des Modes*. Nast renamed the American version *La Gazette du Bon Genre*. Two years later, he bought *L'Illustration des Modes* as well, renaming it *Le Jardin des Modes*. Part of the agreement was that Vogel stay on to run the new magazine as editor-in-chief, with his wife, Cosette, as fashion editor and his brother-in-law, Michel de Brunhoff, as artistic director. Vogel employed the photographic skills of the Seeberger brothers and several of his favourite illustrators – Martin, Marty, Barbier and Brissaud. He also introduced a number of new artists to fashion illustration, notably Mario Simon, Eric, Jacques Demachy, Pierre Mourgue and Helen Smith, many of whom later became famous working for the Condé Nast flagship, *Vogue*.

Also in 1920, a new French magazine, *Art-Goût-Beauté*, began publication with tipped-in pochoir fashion illustrations capturing the unique, young spirit of the changing Art Deco period. Known as *AGB*, it was available in an English-language version to take advantage of the British and American markets. Two years later, another luxurious pochoir

ABOVE LEFT Anni Offterdinger, *Styl*, pochoir over scraperboard, 1923
ABOVE & RIGHT Anni Offterdinger, *Styl*, pochoir over lithograph, 1922

LEFT   Richard Blank, *Styl*, pochoir over lithograph, 1923

RIGHT   *Styl*, pochoir over lithograph, 1924

magazine appeared. Published out of Berlin – by that time an impossibly chic, daring and rather edgy city – *Styl* was an expensive, limited edition magazine, published by Erich Reiss and Otto Von Holten. Its full title was *STYL: Blätter für Mode und die angenehmen Dinge des Lebens* or, roughly translated, *Style: Fashion and the Good Things in Life.*

In Germany, the carnage of the First World War and the subsequent economic collapse of industry gave rise to the design principles of the Bauhaus, led by Walter Gropius and his group of teachers and technicians at the Weimar School of Art. With the painters Wassily Kandinsky and Paul Klee and a number of designers and craftsmen, Gropius began to evolve a theory of modern design based on new technology. It was to be entirely functional in concept and free of superfluous decoration. Its aesthetic appeal would rely solely on the balance and proportion of the component parts and their relationship to the object's intended use. The theories developed at the Bauhaus, with their emphasis on *sachlichkeit* ('matter-of-factness') led to a search for a peculiarly German form of pared-down functionality, a rational mode of design that would be beautiful in its simplicity. Since Germany's very survival depended on rebuilding a manufacturing base, such a recipe for producing simpler goods at lower cost, yet still attractive to consumers, became a cause, almost a cult, and designers devoted themselves to it with great determination.

In France, manufacturing had been almost completely destroyed, with much of the machinery having been looted or converted to armaments. The French were, therefore, unable to concentrate on mass production. Fortunately, the luxury trades, by tradition situated mainly in Paris, remained virtually untouched, and so for France it became economically imperative to build on their reputation as the global capital of fashion and luxury goods. French designers and manufacturers decided to present themselves to the world as the best equipped producers of luxurious and extravagant merchandise and the major Paris fashion houses and ateliers became the principal suppliers of these offerings.

By 1925, the year of the great Art Deco exhibition, the best of the fashion illustrators had moved as far from the imitative, photographic style of drawing as was possible. The inventiveness of these artists in composing the right style and setting for their pochoir illustrations had a distinct influence on Art Deco design, affecting not only the couturiers, who were always ready to pick up on the latest nuances and variations, but also the designers of furniture, textiles, carpets, ceramics and all manner of other items.

Much of the bold splendour of the original forms of Art Deco was, by 1925, being replaced by a more commercial version aimed at the

RIGHT Gerda Wegener, *The Rape of the Lock* from *The Sketch*, photogravure, 1925

The Rape of the Lock.

HAIR-CUT AND SHAVE—NEW VERSION

Drawn by Gerda Wegener.

Nº 213. — Octobre 1928   REVUE MENSUELLE   Le Nº France : 9 francs

La femme chic

NUMÉRO SPÉCIAL DES MODES D'HIVER

Publications A. LOUCHEL   47, Rue de Sèvres, PARIS (6e)

burgeoning market. The style began to lose its identity, becoming more superficial, resulting in the introduction of Jazz Age patterning – an ad hoc mix of visual ideas that today are best described as 1920s kitsch. The Exposition Internationale des Arts Décoratifs et Industriels Modernes was finally held on the banks of the Seine from April to October 1925, with exhibits from twenty-eight other nations, including Russia, Italy, America, Britain, Holland, Turkey and Spain. To showcase the Pavilion de l'Elégance, where the grand couturiers were showing their work, eight pochoir fashion illustrations were created for a special issue of *La Gazette du Bon Ton.* Called the 'Golden Edition', this was to be one of the last appearances of this beautiful magazine, which had done so much to establish the aesthetic integrity of the original Art Deco style and that of fashion illustrators between its first appearance in November 1912 and its final issue in November 1925. Today, each issue is an expensive, highly sought collector's item.

On looking through the glossy fashion magazines of the period, one is above all struck by the simplicity of line of those young ladies with their short, tubular dresses, cloche hats, bobbed hair and assorted bands of bracelets – the symbols of their generation. In the autumn of 1928, for the first time in the recorded history of the western world, young women's knees became an accepted and respectable sight in fashionable society. Introduced as a result of an American dance craze, the Charleston, and featured in that year's hit movie, *Our Dancing Daughters,* starring Joan Crawford as a flapper – a sort of Jazz Age good-time girl – the look sparked new styles in lingerie, decorative garters and knee blush. For the fashionable men of this period, the magazine *Monsieur,* with its wonderful pochoir covers, was of special interest – menswear was, as it always seemed to be, pure English Savile Row with a dash of Paris, to be worn accompanied by, very importantly, the latest motor car and the hottest jazz.

On Wall Street in October 1929, the music suddenly stopped and the dancing ground to a halt. The Charleston, the flappers, the bright and the beautiful were suddenly faced with ugly reality. On 'Black Tuesday' vast fortunes were lost overnight and confusion and uncertainty spread, like a tidal wave, across America and out across the rest of the world – a grim introduction to a new era.

CHAPTER SIX
THE END OF AN EPOCH

Spring 1930 introduced Hollywood's take on the new 'streamlined' look. It would become the style of the decade, defining the thirties in everything from clothes to trains and household appliances. Promoted by most of the British and American fashion magazines, these streamlined collections proclaimed that the crisp, angular, colourful fashions of the 1920s were 'dead, dead, dead'. As one editorial put it, 'How exciting it would be if only we could be naked with a cheque book. To be able to start from scratch at the beginning of this new decade and be able to put on nothing but the new, New, NEW.'

The Paris fashion collections for autumn 1929 anticipated the changes ahead. They dropped hemlines and reintroduced the waist, creating a sensation after years of above-the-knee skirts and the waist-at-the-hips silhouette. It was reported that 'all the women were squirming about in their chairs, tugging at the hem of their skirts at the Patou and Chanel collections.' None of the new-style photographic fashion magazines had been able to predict such a change, as the majority no longer employed the services of innovative fashion illustrators, who in the past had both recorded and predicted fashion trends. Then came October and Black Tuesday. The market crashed from its dizzy heights and everything changed.

For many, during the next few years, Hollywood films would become the great fashion predictors. Until 1929, film companies paid scant attention to fashion, with actresses often supplying their own clothes for contemporary productions. In 1930, when the pictures made just before the crash were released, they created a great deal of unintended mirth. Actresses, sporting what had been chic and fresh in 1928 and early 1929, complete with rouged knees and low waists,

RIGHT Cover art for *La Femme Chic*, photogravure, 1943

LBERT ORCEL
llier LINE VAUTRIN
su ROUBAUDI

PUBLICATIONS A. LOUCHEL
8, RUE HALÉVY PARIS-IX
(Place de l'Opéra)
NUMÉRO 381 — FÉVRIER 1943
FRANCE : 18 FRANCS

LEFT & RIGHT **American advertisements by Joseph Christian Leyendecker, photogravure, 1930s**

romped across the screen looking old-fashioned and out of date. The financial losses this caused taught Hollywood a valuable lesson and all of the major studios immediately set up costume departments, staffed with talented designers like Adrian, Walter Plunkett, Travis Banton, Milo Anders, Orry-Kelly and many others. During the dark days of the Depression, their creations would be seen by an unprecedented audience, as millions flocked to the new, gloriously decorated 'Picture Palaces', the flickering silver screen providing one of the only escapes – a door to other lands and other dreams.

Fashion conscious women turned to the film designers for their inspiration with Adrian at MGM becoming synonymous with the fashions worn by Greta Garbo, Joan Crawford, Jean Harlow, Norma Shearer, Hedy Lemarr and later Lana Turner. His designs became the styles worn by millions, some becoming fashionable almost overnight. As one movie mogul said at the time, 'Before this, Paris fashions were only available to the wealthy few. Now films reveal new styles to the whole country, which are copied by men and women throughout the land.' Many of these film costumiers, like Adrian, became couturiers in the 'real world' too, while fashion on film taught the public a new visual language, making photography the first choice of many fashions magazines from this point on.

TWO SHILLINGS NETT

Harper's Bazaar

INCORPORATING "VANITY FAIR"

january
1930

RIVIERA
FASHIONS

VIRGINIA WOOLF
ANDRÉ MAUROIS
E. M. DELAFIELD
CHERRY POYNTER

LEFT Léon Benigni, cover art for British
Harper's Bazaar, photogravure, 1930

In 1920, Paul Iribe, sensing that the future of creative fashion was in Hollywood, had left Paris to work with Cecil B. DeMille on his film *Male and Female.* His designs helped make Gloria Swanson a star and went a long way to creating the Hollywood Deco Style, the glorious, glamorous, borderline kitsch that DeMille made full use of in his later epic, *Cleopatra.* In the early 1930s Hollywood-style glamour, as personified by the movie stars, was of major importance in the film and fashion magazines, aided by editors who were able to attract more advertising revenue from the ever increasing number of cosmetics companies.

Fashion illustrators had to try to compete with film and capture the mood, the changing ideals of the readers and the new styles. While a few publications, like *AGB*, were still producing quality pochoir illustrations, others moved to less expensive methods of printing for the body of the magazine, reserving the pochoir colour for special centre-spreads and inserts. But the general public, by now used to moving pictures, film stills and star portraits, was ready for photography in their fashion magazines. Pochoir illustration did continue into the 1930s, even into the early years of the 1940s, but for most mid-range magazines, a mix of photographs with a few half-tone colour illustrations became the norm.

Until the time of the Wall Street Crash, fashion illustrators had been encouraged to undertake a commission as they saw fit, creating an image that reflected their view of the subject and using the technique they thought most suitable. But now, a new breed of magazine editors and art directors would often specify exactly what they wanted and would refuse to accept an illustration if it did not strictly conform to their original brief. The magazines of the early 1930s were being designed by the art directors and editors as a complete ensemble, with as much regard being given to the novelty of the layout, the balancing of the text and the placement of the all important advertisements as was given to the content of the illustrations or the text.

This was in contrast to the ideas and ideals of Lucien Vogel and the other innovative publishing entrepreneurs back in 1912, when the artists themselves were commissioned to design the layout and decide the subject of their illustrations. Those artists created the mood for the magazine and in many cases designed the objects or clothes being featured. But in 1932, two events signaled the end of this special era in the history of fashion illustration – the closure of *AGB*'s specialist pochoir studio and the death of George Barbier. By 1933, *Vogue* and several other magazines were also signaling the end of the reign of the illustrator when they began to use photographic covers, one of the first being *Vogue*'s bathing beauty cover, photographed by Edward

ABOVE British fashion magazine illustration, photogravure, mid-1930s

ABOVE Illustration for British magazine by Eric Frazer, photogravure, 1931

Steichen. This was their first photo cover since 1909, and within a few months most other magazines followed suit. At first, the photo covers were a great novelty, but within the year, although they served the magazines well enough, few were really memorable.

Commercialized forms of fashion photography began to thrive. The consummate professionalism of Steichen, Horst P. Horst and Baron Hoyningen-Huene produced inventive images that generally proved to be a very persuasive commercial argument in favour of the use of photographs. And readers liked looking at these images, especially the few that were printed in colour, because they could now more easily identify with the image of a real object, rather than with an illustrative interpretation that often presented an idiosyncratic point of view. During the 1920s, de Meyer and Steichen developed original techniques and an eye for capturing something of the mystery and illusion of the clothes and the women they photographed, but what they could never show was the glimpse of the future that was the special gift of the experienced fashion illustrator. This exclusive, intuitive ability, such as was possessed by the likes of George Barbier or Charles Martin, came from being

American menswear fashion illustrations by Robert Goodman (ABOVE LEFT), Leslie Saalburg (ABOVE) and Laurence Fellows (RIGHT), photogravure, 1930s

Avril 1933   Le N°: **5**ᶠʳˢ FRANCE   13ᵉ Année — N° 152

A̲ʀᴛ · G̲ᴏ̂ᴜᴛ · B̲ᴇᴀᴜᴛᴇ́

FEUILLETS DE L'ÉLÉGANCE FÉMININE
27, RUE DES JEUNEURS
PARIS

LEFT *Art-Goût-Beauté*, coloured lithograph, *c.*1933

ABOVE Régis Manset, cover for the final edition of *Art-Goût-Beauté*, coloured lithograph, 1933

ABOVE & RIGHT *Art-Goût-Beauté*, coloured lithograph, 1930s

ÉDITIONS
ART·GOUT·BEAUTÉ
27, RUE DES JEUNEURS

LEFT Charles Martin, *Art-Goût-Beauté*, coloured lithograph, 1930
RIGHT Gaston Maréchaux, *Art-Goût-Beauté*, hand-coloured pochoir, 1930s

able to first distil the mood of the day, *l'air du temps*, the zeitgeist of the moment, and then to draw out of that, literally, the signs and beginnings of tomorrow's trends.

For a short time, an attempt was made to capture this missing element. Fashion editors and their photographers started to demand that they have dresses specially made in advance of their general release for sale. By the mid-1930s, a visitor to Rome after Christmas may well have seen models, shivering on the Spanish Steps, being photographed in what a magazine's editor thought would be next spring's clothes. This meant that these new fashions had to be invented especially for photographic shoots, although they were often quite unlike the designs that did then become fashionable. This had the effect of forcing designers to 'fly a kite' (to use a design created especially for publicity purposes) or of making photographers place more emphasis on novelty accessories, unusual locations and the

JANVIER 1935

VOICI LA MODE

**ART
GOUT
BEAUTE**

CHANEL

Manteau bleu vif, doublé de tussor rouge imprimé d'un semis blanc, bleu et noir semblable à la robe.

PRIX : 4 FRANCS

lbénigni

PUBLIÉ A PARIS PAR LES ÉDITIONS ÉDOUARD BOUCHERIT

LEFT Léon Benigni, cover art for *Voici La Mode*, photogravure, 1935

photogenic qualities of the model rather than the clothing. Although this tended to slow down and distort the fashions of the period, there were nevertheless some very fine images published in the mid- to late 1930s. As had happened with the inventive fashion illustrations of the mid-nineteenth century, these photographs eventually began to influence the actual fashions being worn.

For the majority of fashion illustrators of the mid-1930s, there were other concerns. Most magazines were now essentially advertising vehicles, so the bulk of the work available was for manufacturers, department stores or catalogues. This often called for 'grafting bizarre details and a modern face on to an already outdated advertisement', according to Eliot Hodgkin, author of *Fashion Drawing*, a book that details many of the fashion drawing techniques of the 1930s. He went on to say that in the advertiser's mind 'every woman is supposed to be chronically dissatisfied with her figure and incapable of altering it' so an illustrator 'must show Mrs Everyman as she would appear after putting on a magic dress that makes her delightfully slender'. With both editors and advertisers dictating content, there was very little room for idiosyncrasy or creativity and most illustrations became, consequently, rather mundane. The quid pro quo agreement that had developed between the fashion magazines and the advertisers quickly led to their becoming stereotyped and boring.

Only Lucien Vogel's French magazine, *Le Jardin des Modes*, and French *Vogue* under the direction of his brother-in-law, Michel de Brunhoff, seem to have been free of this heavy-handedness. Their circulations began to increase until even their competitors were forced to give a freer rein to their illustrators, allowing them to draw the sorts of images for which they had originally become famous. The editors had forgotten that a fashion magazine should not simply catalogue the available; its essential role should be one of experimentation and prediction. As one commentator wrote: 'Even the marginal *croquis* and vignettes supplied by minor, perhaps anonymous artists, often point to the mood and spirit of the particular moment with the poignancy that photographs could never match. There is no more potent agent of recall than the illustrated magazine, which designed to catch the passing moment on the wing, thus unselfconsciously, almost absently stores it away to mature as it may . . . And where it is the artist who supplies its images, the substance is more particular, more personal, more piquant, for he or she cannot just accept, but must absorb and process it all, through the senses and imagination, and every mark becomes a kind of declaration.'

In 1933, *Art-Goût-Beauté* ceased publication. The previous year it had changed format, introducing litho illustrations and photographs

LEFT Etienne Drian, photogravure,
*c.*1935
RIGHT French magazine illustration,
photogravure, 1930

of their sponsoring couturiers' collections. After 152 issues, it finally changed both its format and name, becoming *Voici La Mode* – a near lookalike of Lucien Vogel's *Le Jardin des Modes*. The pochoir was gone, replaced by standard photo-mechanically printed fashion illustrations by anonymous artists. It reflected the look of the glamorous Hollywood stars of the period – Marlene Dietrich, Greta Garbo, Joan Crawford, Norma Shearer, Claudette Colbert and Ruby Keeler. Things had come full circle. Paris had sent its ideas of beauty and elegance out into the world for generations; now trends were set on sound stages in California and flooded across movie screens, changing fashion faster, and more widely, than could ever have been imagined.

LEFT British magazine illustration, photogravure, 1935

RIGHT French magazine illustration by Giron, photogravure, mid-1930s

Many of the other popular, established magazines adapted themselves to the change of pace with much the same mix of photographs and attractive, colourful, often unattributed fashion illustration. Pochoir survived as the preferred printing method for the more exclusive print jobs, with ateliers in Vienna doing the best work, producing biannual editions of *Wiener Mode Kunst* and other high quality fashion pochoir and refined ten-colour litho folders such as *Elégances du Soir*, *Les Grands Modeles* and *Les Croquis du Grand Chic* – all keeping alive the spirit and the style of the short-lived but influential *Styl* magazine of the early 1920s. In Germany and Austria, fashion magazines like *Deutsche Moden-Zeitung*, *Wiener Mode*, *Wiener Damenmode* and the glossy *Iris* were popular. A cultural difference was beginning to become apparent on the pages of these publications. While American, British and French fashion was being increasingly influenced by Hollywood, German and Austrian designers were looking for inspiration closer to home. Germany may have rebuilt itself after the First World War with the help of idealists like Walter Gropius and his Bauhaus international style, but by the early 1930s, traditional German art and design were back in popular

LEFT *La Femme Chic*, photogravure, 1930s
RIGHT Pierre Mourgue, *La Gazette du Bon Ton*, hand-coloured pochoir, mid-1920s

and political favour. On assuming power, the Nazi government founded a German fashion institute, the Deutsches Modeamt, to encourage the German fashion industry and designers. Traditional, regional costume or Tracht, with dirndl skirts, embroidered bodices and Tyrol jackets, was encouraged. The main aim of the institute however, was to erase French influence on German fashion. In 1933, Hitler himself proclaimed, 'No more Paris fashions.' He had hopes that Berlin would one day be the fashion capital of the world and later, when France fell, Joseph Goebbels allowed and endorsed the creation of luxurious German high fashion publications, such as *Die Grosse Modes*, with hand-coloured illustrations.

Meanwhile, in America and the rest of Europe, the Depression slowly began to lift, and by the mid-1930s the major Parisian couturiers

were at last being regularly patronized by a steady flow of customers from all over the world. These individuals were willing and able to pay Paris prices, particularly for glamorous evening dresses. Couture customers, it was noted, were younger than in the days before the crash and they preferred figure-hugging clothes, cut on the bias *à la Vionnet*. Influenced by stars like Jean Harlow, customers demanded more daring designs, wanting to show what had previously been concealed and encouraging designers to create more revealing styles. Lingerie, if it was worn at all, became important, having to be as beautifully cut as the dresses themselves so as not to spoil the line.

Outside of the couture houses, however, many of the major design commissions were now coming from public or commercial clients rather than individuals. Hollywood Deco was inspiring the

Heft 1

V

14 täglich 75 Rpf.
einschließlich 5 Rpf. Bestellgeld.
Zuschlag gemäß aufsichts-
behördlicher Anordnung 10 Rpf.
85 Rpf.

Deutsche
Moden-
Zeitung
vereinigt mit Beyers Modenblatt
Frau·Volk·Welt

K 22360

51. Jahrgang
1 9 4 1
Leipzig / Oktober
14 täglich ein Heft
Verlagsort Leipzig

Verlag Otto Beyer
Leipzig – Berlin

LEFT Cover art for *Deutsche Moden-Zeitung*, coloured lithograph, 1941
RIGHT Eduardo García Benito, *Album de Figaro*, photogravure, 1943

AGNÈS
*Turban de jersey
Oiseau multicolore*

SYGUR
*Velours violet
et bouquet de roses*

JANETTE COLOMBIER
*Velours rubis
et plumes de coq*

LES

Benito

design of gorgeously glamorous cinemas across the USA and Britain. Radio City Music Hall in New York was a monument to the modern style. Perhaps the greatest official commission of this period was for the fitting out of the French luxury liner, SS *Normandie*. The ship was designed to be the most beautiful ever built and to give every passenger the feeling of luxurious elegance normally only experienced by movie stars and millionaires. *Normandie* would also be a showcase for French design, craftsmanship and style. In her every detail, a magnificent tribute to the greatest decorative artists of French Art Deco – Jean Dunand, Eugene Rodier, Jean Dupas among others – *Normandie* was advertising on a grand scale. Launched in 1935, the liner quickly became the most fashionable and luxurious way to travel. Americans flocked to Paris and London to see what the great dress-makers and tailors had to offer. The following year, travel between the continents became both quicker and easier with airlines

LEFT Domenique, *Le Bonheur du Jour*, pochoir and lithograph, 1944
ABOVE Etienne Drian, photogravure, *c.*1929

extending their services with a 32-seat Fokker XXXVI and the new Empire flying boat; the *Queen Mary* made her maiden voyage to New York; and the newest German airship, the Zeppelin *Hindenburg*, was coming into regular service – Frankfurt to Lakehurst, New Jersey, in forty-eight hours, Frankfurt to Rio in eighty and San Francisco to Manila in fifty-eight.

Unfortunately, competition between nations was not confined to matters of style and travel. Between 1936 and 1939, the Spanish Civil War, the Italian conquest of Ethiopia, troubles in Greece and Yugoslavia, Hitler's actions at home, in the Rhineland and Poland, all made for grim headlines. In New York, the International Exhibition or World's Fair, in planning since 1935, opened in April 1939, but by August, with the invasion of Poland and Germany's refusal to back down, war in Europe was openly declared and the atmosphere between the various national pavilions became, to say the least, tense.

In spite of war, in early 1940, Paris presented its spring fashion collections, which were said to be a 'triumph of taste' as well as a 'triumph of courage'. Considered to be of such immense importance, the fashion industry represented a huge annual turnover (in the region of 28 billion francs) and employed a large and highly specialized workforce. The French government, with 'great imagination, released on leave [*permission* in French] the fashion designers, who created the collections in a fortnight, and the accessory makers, who did their job and then returned to the front. The new fashions were designed with serious devotion, as befits a serious industry, which is the life-blood of French exports.' The press photographers and fashion illustrators, it was reported, willingly gave up their periods of leave to promote the collections, prompting the nickname of *Les Collections des Permissionnaires*. The dress shows were 'colourful, but not gaudy; rich, but not ostentatious; gay, but not frivolous'. It was the given job of the fashion illustrators to add the necessary glamour to this rushed but important collection and many would continue to do so over the course of the war in ways photographers never could.

Films during the war, especially when paper supplies were restricted and distribution impossible, had an enormous influence on the development of fashion, even if wartime conditions made those styles difficult to find or make. In one magazine in 1940, the Hollywood film *The Women* was recommended to its readers as being almost essential viewing. The featured clothes, designed by the famous costumier Adrian, were described as having a 'luxurious yet appealing air' and it was claimed, 'Gone forever are the days when it was wrong for a woman to make the most of herself, with cosmetics, an attractive figure and beautiful clothes. More than ever in these dull, anxious war

ABOVE **Pierre Mourgue**, *La Femme Chic*, photogravure, 1944

RIGHT **Pierre Louchel**, *La Femme Chic*, photogravure, 1943

LEFT Pierre Mourgue, *La Femme Chic*,
photogravure, 1942
ABOVE Pierre Louchel, *La Femme Chic*,
photogravure, 1943

days it has become the duty, as well as the pleasure of women to make themselves good to look at.' Looking back at Adrian's designs for that remarkable film, one can see the full range of 1940s fashion details – from square shoulders and short skirts to the first hints of what would be reworked by Dior in 1947 as the New Look.

With the wartime situation worsening, news came about the fall of France and, as the bombing of London and other major cities began, the role of the fashion illustrators, at least in Britain, must have seemed fairly redundant. Outside of the cinema, despite the government's insistence on a good appearance as a morale booster, most fashion advice, even in British *Vogue*, was of the 'make do and mend' variety. Clothing rationing was strict, raw materials hard to get. Rationing was also in effect in France and, as the the Germans occupied Paris and the Vichy government got ready to promote its vision of a more solid and homely French woman, it seemed that it would be difficult to keep the torch of chic burning. Several fashion houses closed their doors or moved away, and those that remained, along with the surviving ateliers, faced a hard struggle to keep going in the face of a shrinking market, lack of raw materials and a reduced workforce. On the whole, it is remarkable that so many fashion publishers continued to produce magazines throughout the war in France, bolstering the vestiges of haute couture by featuring articles on each season's new styles, illustrated with drawings and photographs. Towards the end of 1942, some of the more expensive fashion goods became difficult to find and there was an appreciable lowering of quality in what was available.

The press in Britain and America was asked to co-operate with their governments in reducing consumer demand for many items. One of the greatest problems at the time was fabric supply and it became the subject of many editorials, impressing on readers the necessity to rethink and reduce their wardrobes, many assuring readers that it would be a good thing for a good cause: 'It is generally agreed that variety has run riot of recent years. In the past it's been too easy to confuse variety with excellence . . . personally we would sacrifice variety and style in the hope that this will reflect in new trends. We do not believe this will stifle creative enterprise.' In magazines and pamphlets, diagrams and drawings showed women how best to reuse or make practical clothing and it was here that fashion illustrators could gloss over the unpicked, recut garments, imbuing them with a little much needed magic.

In America, designers were encouraged to step into the gap left by the lack of access to French couture and they began to develop styles that could be adapted to sell to everyone, not just the wealthy.

RIGHT Pierre Louchel, *La Femme Chic*, photogravure, 1943

ABOVE **Pierre Louchel**, *La Femme Chic*, photogravure, 1944

These new designs were promoted by talented and highly skilled fashion illustrators, some of whom had left Europe for New York at the outbreak of war. Back in Britain, the government had just banned silk stockings and the news that American girls were sporting the latest fashion invention, nylon stockings, caused envy and a future black market boom. The British Board of Trade introduced 'utility clothing', which was intended to be simple, practical and inexpensive and as good looking and agreeable to wear as was possible, given the limited resources available. They co-opted the services of many of the country's leading designers – Edward Molyneux, Hardy Amies, Digby Morton to name just a few – to help make the project a success.

By now, most of France was affected by cuts and shortages and clothes rationing too. Only in Paris and Lyon did the fashion industry continue to operate. The seasonal couture collections continued to be shown, as did the art of the creative fashion illustrators like Pierre Mourgue, René Gruau, Jacques Demachy, André Delfau, Ettiene Drian, Georges and Claude Lepape, Eduardo García Benito, Bernard

ABOVE Pierre Louchel, *La Femme Chic*, photogravure, 1943

Blossac, plus Jean Cocteau and a number of others who promoted the seasonal collections of the couturiers who stayed in business – Jean Patou, Lanvin, Jeanne Paquin, Maggy Rouff, Balanciaga, Jacques Fath and Lucien Lelong – and continued as if, according to critics, 'the war didn't exist'. Hitler's plan had been to move the entire Paris fashion world to Berlin. But, when it was realized that this would involve relocating over 10,000 atelier workers, their families, the suppliers, plus all of the ancillary trades, the plan was shelved and the Parisian fashion business was left to continue almost as before.

Despite the fact that the designers and fashion illustrators often used the patriotic red, white and blue, including a suggestion of resistance in the themes and backgrounds of their illustrations, people outside of France were shocked when they eventually got to see fashion magazines from Paris, in which the French appeared to have what they had not. Michel de Brunhoff, who had left at the outbreak of war, and Elsa Schiaparelli, who was in America at the time raising money for French charities, tried, rather in vain, to present it as French fashion's determined and particular fight against the Nazi occupiers, to explain that the wearing of large and jaunty hats and pretty clothes was the French woman's way of showing contempt for her oppressor. As Schiaparelli said, 'In difficult times, fashion is always outrageous.' But the facts seen by the outside world remained – the Paris fashion magazines continued to review collection after collection from all of the above-named designers and others like Schiaparelli, Molyneux, Worth and Bruyère, who were all still open for business. The magazines were still filled with advertising for furs, cosmetics, perfumes and all manner of luxury items. After the outraged public reaction, and especially after the Liberation of Paris in 1944, great care was taken to censor news about Paris fashions, to quash rumours of collaboration and excess.

After the excitement and emotion of the liberation and the final end to the war in Europe in 1945, the process of rebuilding a fashion industry in Paris began in earnest. In Britain, rationing would stay in force until the 1950s, and America's native designers and manufacturers who had taken advantage of the hiatus to siphon off some of the market were busily establishing a fashionable American ready-to-wear industry. For the French it was imperative that they get one of their most essential industries firmly established again. Every tool available would be pressed into this service, most particularly those of the fashion image-makers, the illustrators. Paris counted on women being sick of austerity and making do. The press was bored too, and now that the need to tow a government line was ended, they were eager for something to write about. Only in Britain, where the new Labour government maintained rationing and an embargo on imported fashion, were journalists asked to continue to 'balance' editorial content and to 'prove conclusively' that London fashion was not only reviving but thriving.

By February 1947, however, there was only one fashion story that counted – the success of the newly founded House of Dior. Christian Dior, who had been Lucien Lelong's chief design assistant through the war years, opened his own couture house. Backed by the textile manufacturer Marcel Boussac, Dior attracted instant and international acclaim. Aware that the fashion business was changing, his idea was to showcase his new season collections and then sell each design as *toiles* or patterns to manufacturers around the world, allowing for the mass production of couture-like designer clothes. His idea was a brilliant one. The 'Corolle' line, which would soon be dubbed Dior's 'New Look', was to make the front page of newspapers around the world. Photographs and descriptions of these extravagant, long and full-skirted designs caused a sensation. The shooting of publicity photographs on the streets of Montmartre resulted in the mannequins being attacked, as outraged women tore the dresses from their backs. In Britain, the government considered emergency laws against these 'wasteful', almost ankle length, full skirts, while American ladies formed 'a little below the knee' clubs as a protest against Dior's latest style. Such negative publicity was gold and eventually, although some held out against it, the New Look won out.

This new fashion business model went from strength to strength. Increased production brought designer touches to even the most modest store-bought wardrobe and fashion magazines increasingly reflected a wider and less rarefied readership. Mass-produced fashion meant increased advertising and advertising meant persuasive advertising budgets, and while illustration was still important, photography was proving increasingly popular with advertisers and editors. Illustration, as ever a commercial art, would survive and continue but the ethos that had fueled the halcyon days, when artists had free rein to create high fashion fantasies for the likes of *La Galerie des Modes* or *La Gazette du Bon Ton*, had changed.

And so this is where our story ends, at a point where the world, at peace after yet another 'war to end all wars', begins to shrink as planes, trains, ships and cars link people ever more quickly and easily around the globe, unifying fashion and taste. And from here, looking back, we see our long line of gifted artists, some remembered and many whose names were never known – stretching all the way back to Dürer, the artists of the ancient world and beyond to the prehistoric rock painters. Working artists all, who, hand in hand with other

RIGHT   Pierre Louchel, *La Femme Chic*, photogravure, 1944

PUBLICATIONS A. LOUCHEL
8, RUE HALÉVY — PARIS-IX°
(Place de l'Opéra)

REVUE MENSUELLE
NUMÉRO 400 — DÉCEMBRE 1944
FRANCE : 40 FRANCS

PUBLICATION PÉRIODIQUE

NUMÉRO SPÉCIAL

LEFT Pierre Louchel, *La Femme Chic*,
photogravure, 1944

talented artisans, produced magic, ultimately leading to today's multi-billion-dollar fashion magazine industry.

It is unfortunate that, despite its long heritage, certain prejudices have for too long determined how we rate creativity in this area. One is that fashion and, by extension, fashion illustration is still regarded as being somehow lightweight, not a serious art form. Then there is the notion that the work of the commercial, paid-by-the-job artist is somehow not 'true' art. This attitude has led fashion illustration to be viewed through the wrong end of the telescope – making it seem small, less important, inconsequential. It is a ridiculous distinction. These illustrators have had an impact on a far wider audience than many a 'fine' artist could even imagine, let alone hope to reach. Far from being simply a promotional or advertising tool, their skills have been understood and put to use by monarchs, politicians, dictators and philosophical movers and shakers to help effect great social and economic change.

Despite this, little thought has been given by historians to the influence of the 400-year rise of fashion illustration and magazines, journals, broadsheets and books that developed to feed our aesthetic curiosity, reflecting the visual inventiveness of the people of their day. A great number of the freedoms we take for granted began with them, starting a process that would change much more than the clothes we wore, the food we ate or the music and media we consumed to inform and entertain ourselves. It would alter how we chose to live, transforming our ideals, ideas and aspirations beyond the wildest imaginings of past generations. Whether we are concious of or acknowledge it, we as a culture are indebted to the illustrators and artists of the past for our visual and aesthetic heritage. We are more literate, more affluent and more equal than ever before. We live in an age where television and, to a rapidly increasing extent, the Internet influence our lives. We have access to fashion imagery from any part of the globe at the touch of a button and the freedom to buy and wear whatever we choose, from any country and any culture that appeals and make it our own. Dürer, Vecellio and all the other artists whose work fill these pages would be proud.

LIST OF ILLUSTRATIONS

RIGHT   Lutz Ehrenberger, *Styl*, hand-coloured pochoir, 1923

INDEX

Page numbers in *italic* type refer to the captions to the illustrations

Frances Lincoln Limited
74–77 White Lion Street
London N1 9PF
www.franceslincoln.com

FRONT COVER George Barbier, *La Gazette du Bon Ton*, hand-coloured pochoir, 1921

BACK COVER Claude-Louis Desrais, *La Galerie des Modes*, hand-coloured

copperplate engraving, 1778

HALF TITLE PAGE Harrison Fisher, *An American Beauty*, photogravure, 1909

TITLE PAGE Pierre Louchel, *La Femme Chic*, photogravure, 1943